To Fetch a Pail of Water
REVISITED
...with a Few Pails More
A Story of Water in Lincoln City

By TREVOR E PACEY

To Fetch a Pail of Water

First Published in 1998 by Trevor Pacey
This edition published in 2011 © Tucann *books*

ISBN 978-1-907516-15-3

Text © Trevor Pacey 2011
Design © TUCANN*books* 2011

All rights reserved. No part of this publication may be reproduced or transmitted in any way or by any means, including electronic storage and retrieval, without prior permission of the author.

Produced by: TUCANN*books*, 19 High Street, Heighington, Lincoln LN4 1RG
Tel and Fax: 01522 790009
Website. www.tucann.co.uk

Acknowledgements

There are so many people I wish to thank, for information I have received / acquired / collected during the cause of the three years in writing this book. Without your help this book could not have been written, may I just say many thanks to each of you.

I would like to pass on a special thank you to.....
(The Late) Mr Laurence Elvin, for his help and invaluable guidance.
(The Late) Mr Tom Baker, for his Historical Knowledge of Lincoln.
Mr Maurice Hodson, for his help with information and many photographs.
Helena Nannastead, for guiding me to information at the Local Studies Library of Lincolnshire.
    Also for having photographs reproduced from the Local Studies Collection.

Thank you to many ex-colleagues and friends at Anglian Water for information, help, memories and photographs.
In particular to Mr Paul Valleley Director of Water Services
Thanks also to Mr E Newton, Mr R Dickson, Mr G Clarke, Mr B Vear, Mr A Creasey, Mr E White, Mrs J Brown, Mr C Graby, Mrs L Graby and Mrs M Wareham.

And Finally Mr D J Willington of Harrow, Middlesex. Who is the Great, Great Grandson of Henry Teague the first Water Engineer for Lincoln in 1846.

Introduction

Water, as with so many things today, is taken for granted. We turn on the tap and rightfully expect water to flow, we expect it to be clean, healthy and flowing freely. Only in times of draught or breakdown, when little flows, do we jolt and think maybe supplies are not as plentiful or reliable after all.

This book tells the story of how Lincoln people, from its Roman begins, to the Modern City, created and equipped themselves with a water supply to bring life to their City.

Many devices, methods and sources were used and some failures and many successes were experienced, many good times, some tragic times, are all discussed in this fascinating account.

This Story is told as near to factual as research permits, but some assumptions have had to be made at times, to enhance that Historical Era and to allow an interesting story to be told.

You will observe from the start and as the story develops, how two items are common place throughout nearly 2000 years of Lincoln's Water Supply, one is The River Witham, always useful, but often the Villain and the Second an item, always useful and found to be the best stand-by item for any water system, particularly in the case of a water leak or as a water carrier, the Bucket or The ever present One Gallon PAIL of WATER.

And How This Book Came About?

As a boy at Westgate School in Lincoln, I would stand looking up at this huge building almost in the school grounds, this building was the Water Tower, later on a school trip, I stood in amazement at the workings of Lincoln's water Engine's, this would appear to be it, but as my career developed I find myself not only employed by the Company that owned these, but in charge of the operation of Lincoln's Water Supplies.

This story, to the best of my knowledge, has never been told and I wonder why?

It is interesting, it is fascinating and it tells of areas in Lincoln, you may think, Oh that's what that was for, or that's where that name came from, or just what a lot of trouble people go to, just to get a drink of water.

I hope you enjoy reading it as much as I have enjoyed, over the last 3 years, writing it and **any profits made from its purchase will go to Water Aid**, a charity that supports the not so fortunate areas in the World where good water is not so available, or as healthy, but is as anywhere, necessary for life itself.

Preface
To Fetch a Pail of Water revisited with a Few Pails More. A story of water in Lincoln City

By Trevor E Pacey

In celebration of The CENTENARY of a safe and consistent drinking water.

It has been 12 years since 'To Fetch a Pail of Water' was first published, many have requested a second publication after the first edition sold out and until now that hasn't been realistic, but 2011 is a significant year in the history of water supplies in Lincoln City, so a republication seemed appropriate.

A centenary celebration is to take place in October 2011, organised by The Rotary Club of Lincoln with the full support and expertise of Anglian Water along with various very generous sponsors. All the profits from book sales and the centenary day will go to Water Aid. In particular to those less fortunate than ourselves in areas where fresh water supplies are scarce and difficult to acquire. Also to the Water Aid volunteers supporting the recent disaster areas of the world, in Pakistan, Australia and Japan where drinking water has been so polluted by flooding it has caused severe health problems, serious hardship and the spread of much disease.

This Revisited Book contains a lot of added content to the original and incorporates how water has become more a way of life than ever, how it is used in our everyday lives and how we struggle to cope when suddenly it is either not there or not safe to drink.

To Fetch a Pail of Water

This is the front cover of the 1st issue of 'To Fetch a pail of water' it illustrates how Lincoln City's High Street may have looked in 1910, with the Obelisk on the High Bridge one of several points from where water could be acquired.

Hope you enjoy.

Index

Chapter 1	The Earliest Recollections	Page 1
Chapter 2	Anglo Saxon and Norman Times (5th-11th Century)	Page 5
Chapter 3	Medieval Times (1200-1400s)	Page 7
Chapter 4	The Middle Ages (1500s onwards)	Page 8
Chapter 5	A Waterworks Charter for The City	Page 11
Chapter 6	The Water Undertaking of The City of Lincoln	Page 15
Chapter 7	The Sanitation System.	Page 25
Chapter 8	How Quickly things Change.	Page 29
Chapter 9	The Darkest Days.	Page 32
Chapter 10	A City on the Brink of Disaster.	Page 37
Chapter 11	A Water Tower for the City.	Page 41
Chapter 12	A Reservoir for Quality and Security	Page 46
Chapter 13	A New Source is Born.	Page 52
Chapter 14	The Life Line to the City.	Page 56
Chapter 15	The Heart and Life Blood.	Page 65
Chapter 16	A Little Touch of Brilliance.	Page 76
Chapter 17	The Christening	Page 80
Chapter 18	Deliverance.	Page 84
Chapter 19	The Completion of a Masterpiece.	Page 92
Chapter 20	The Ever Increasing Demand.	Page 97
Chapter 21	Supporting Bomber Command.	Page 105
Chapter 22	The Centenary of the Water Company	Page 110
Chapter 23	The Water Board.	Page 113
Chapter 24	The Awesome Power of Steam	Page 118
Chapter 25	A Water Authority.	Page 122
Chapter 26	Too little or Too much	Page 125
Chapter 27	A few Pails more.	Page 134
Chapter 28	And now its been 100 Years	Page 144
Chapter 29	And Finally	Page 160
References		Page 163

Chapter 1
THE EARLIEST RECOLLECTIONS

This Story begins around 50 AD, for it was around this time The Roman Empire, expanding across Europe and into Britain, began building their settlements. A consideration as to where to build a settlement must have been the availability of food and water, also how plentiful and transportable it was. Fish, it appears, was a Roman favourite along with bread and wine. Transportation was over long, flat and straight roads or by natural waterways and canals, where the waterways had a natural potential, the Romans, would often build their settlements.

Lincolnshire must have been an attraction for it fulfilled most of the criteria. Rising in the South West, close to Grantham, meandering North through the County to the middle at Lincoln, forming a large pool before turning East, then South East to Boston and the Wash, where it flows into the North Sea is the River Witham and this contributed to most of the criteria.

The large pool at Lincoln, Brayford Pool was, seemingly, the ideal place for the early settlement. Recognising it's potential, the Romans dug a Canal from The Brayford Pool, to link with the larger River Trent on the County border with Nottinghamshire, this not only gave them an abundance of food, but also a navigational route across the County and into the Midlands.

As the Roman Colonies expanded so too did their transport routes. The Fosseway passing through Lincoln as it sped from Grimsby across England to the South West and Ermine Street as it crossed The Fosseway at Lincoln on its way from The Great North Road near Peterborough to the River Humber in the North of Lincolnshire, Lincoln or as the Romans called it Lindum Colonial was to be an important area of Roman England.

Most activity in Lincoln was around the Brayford Pool and although fish may have been abundant, good drinking water was not. Water was not so much drunk, but it was essential for brewing and baking and of course for life itself, the Romans were getting most of this water from wells they had dug around the Pool.

As Lindum developed a Garrison was built, it spread along Ermine Street, North East of The Pool, uphill and dry seemed sensible, but further away from the water seemed a puzzle.

Another Canal, The Cardyke, was constructed, to both act as a drainage dyke and in many parts as a navigational waterway. As it carried from the River Witham at Lincoln, through the fertile Fenland, to link with the River Nene. The

To Fetch a Pail of Water

Cardyke had linked the large farming area of the Fens to the Military Garrisons in the North, via Lindum Colonial.

Lincoln was in a prime position as a gateway to the Midlands and North, a larger Garrison was to be built North of the Brayford Pool, this would mean any natural water course was deep below ground and the further up hill, the further away would be the water. So where would the 300 population get their clean water?

The Romans never built a City where water was scarce or difficult to get hold of, Lincoln though, must have caused at least a little scratching of the head!

Water, water everywhere, but not a drop to drink. This seemed to be the case! The River and Canal were for navigational transport, fishing, bathing and perhaps waste disposal, but definitely not for drinking or at least not directly.

Where then was the clean water to come from?

Lindum Colonial as it may have appeared.

Wells were dug into the rocky ridge, much like those around the Brayford Pool, one still being in place in the Bail were Saint Paul's Church once stood, this well has recently been exposed and a showcase covers it so it can be viewed by many passers by, this served the Roman Market Place close to the Roman Forum, but more than wells were required.

Catching rainwater in large storage tanks was another method, but they would still need something that was a little more reliable.

What it appears they did do was this.

A little East of Newport Arch, in East Bight (possibly the highest point in the Roman City), The Romans, built a cistern / water tower (ruins can be viewed

To Fetch a Pail of Water

today) and setting off from the cistern North East along the Fosseway (the A46, Nettleham Road) they built a pipeline, known in Roman Times as a "Conduit". This "Conduit" was made up of earthenware pipes, 1 foot 10 inches long, each being joined, with no insertion, but with a ring of very strong cement. The pipe was then laid very precisely onto a strong cement base, forming a bed for the pipe, and then the whole conduit was encased in the Cement, giving a very strong water tight pipeline.

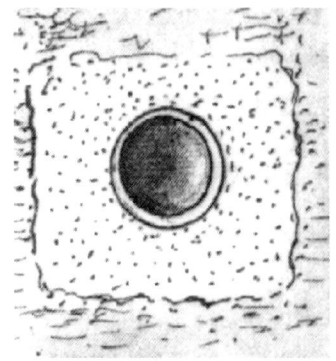

This illustration shows sections of the pipe with its cement casing and the base on which it was laid.

This illustration shows how it was laid below ground and encased totally in a cement block.

The Conduit was laid for over 2000 yards slowly falling from its higher level in the Bail, to terminate close to, todays Outer Circle Road junction with Nettleham Road, North East of Lincoln.

At this point Waitrose Supermarket now occupies this site and here they have a fragment of roman pipe in its jacket of opus siginum (Roman cement) which was found during excavation. Also here is a mosaic, in the foyer, which shows how the Roman system may have worked, there was a fast flowing stream, called the "Roaring Meg", this then was to be the water source.

As this area was around 70 feet below the level of East Bight a means of lifting the water had to be arranged. Did the Romans have Pumps?

The earliest known system must be the Archemedes screw, the quite ingenious, yet very simple rotating twisting spiral, this along with suction pumps (similar in operation to the bicycle pump), driven by animal or man, do go back beyond this date.

A Water Tower with a falling multi arch aqueduct, a notably famous structure in Roman History, was believed to be here. Water was raised (pumped) into this tower from one side out of the Roaring Meg and allowed to fall the other side down another arched aqueduct into the conduit pipeline, therefore, the water, was forced under pressure to supply the Garrison more than a mile away, this was, it seemed a probability, but experts still ponder!

The Roman Cistern would have been at the highest point in the Roman City, so pipework laid from it would allow the water to flow, by gravity, to anywhere within the Roman City. The Roman Forum, bath houses which are believed to have had hot water and fountains were along the main street just a few strides away and could be supplied easily. It is thought a reservoir was also built, close to where the Water Tower stands today near the West Gate.

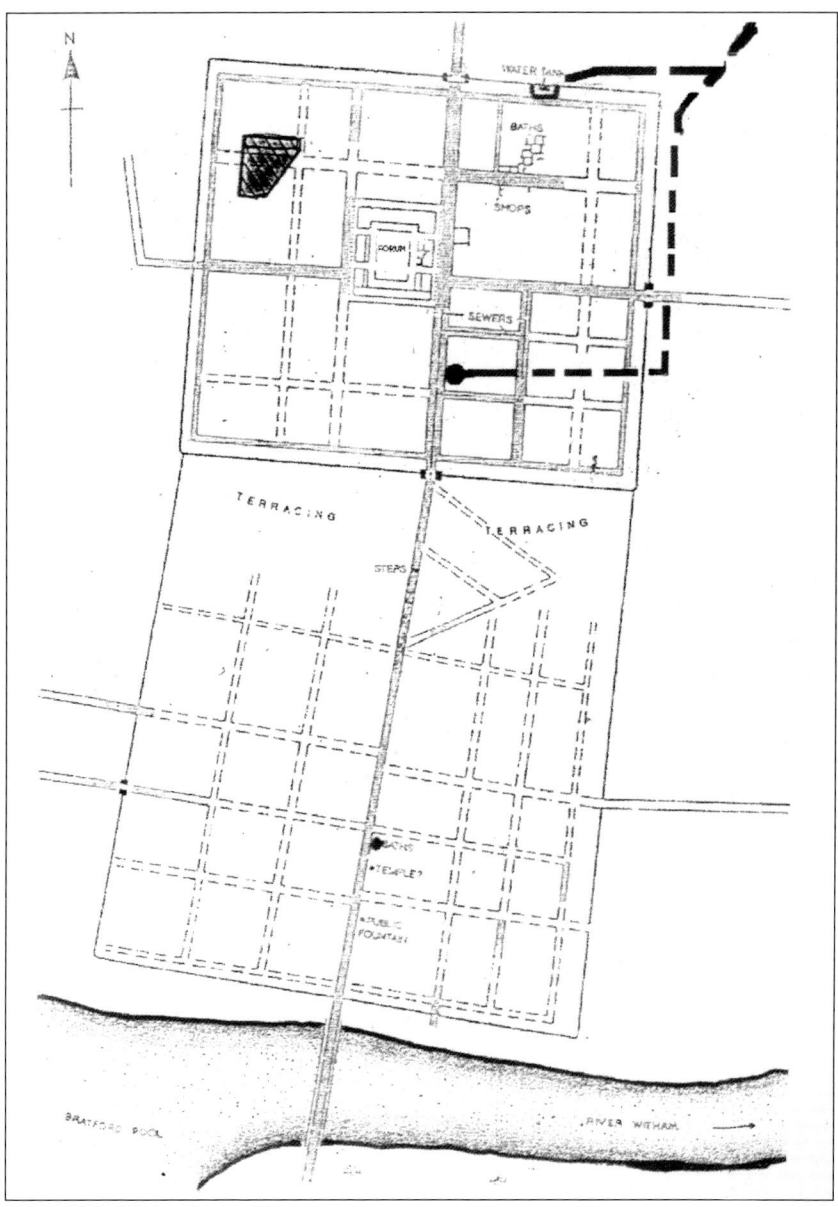

A Plan of the Lindum Roman City

Chapter 2
ANGLO SAXON AND NORMAN TIMES
(5TH-11TH CENTURY)

The City saw many changes to its sky line, but few changes to the water supplies. The drinking water was supplied from seasonal tapped springs and wells dug through the rocky ridge, the collecting of rainwater was another option. The Roman system had disappeared by now, but the Roman Town boundary still held most of the population.

Lincoln was home for between 6-7000 people, they lived mainly in the area North of the Stonebow. Digging of wells was the reliable system for getting drinking water, although catching rainwater was an interesting science, indeed perhaps more gadgets were invented for this, than for raising water from the ground.

Many wells were private others in Newport, The Exchequer Square and Eastgate housed some of the larger public wells.

The Castle came along with the Norman Conquest and at least one well was dug in here! The Cathedral and further wells, this time a small reservoir was built and the water was also used for fire fighting. How accessible these supplies were to the public is unknown, but most of the population were certainly close by.

Many of these wells had hand operated pumps, and a rope and bucket, others had one or the other. At the junction of Langworthgate and Greetwellgate near to Winnowsty Lane, was a popular well, called "The Leadenwell" and it became notorious

A typical well arrangement with its rope and bucket and to the left a typical pump arrangement.

To Fetch a Pail of Water

for its rope and bucket failures, someone would have to climb down the iron ladder inside and recover the bucket each time it failed.

A confined shallow aquifer*, probably of limestone, many feet below, was where the water was drawn from and it would have taken some effort for water to be lifted to the surface in a bucket, so a pump would have been quite useful, but the cost tended to prevent this luxury.

Pumps around this time would be of the simple suction type. A lever cranked up and down could suck water from 20 feet below and (if fitted with a 4 inch barrel, an average size) would draw 9 gallons (41 litres) in a minute, providing 25 strokes of the handle could be managed.

Some time later a throw pump came along, this enabled a vertical wheel to be fitted and a simple spin of the wheel by hand could draw twice as much as its predecessor

*Aquifer a water bearing rock within the strata.

Just off Steep Hill is Well Lane and at it's lower level is a pump and this is probably the well used during the time and it is probable a pump of its kind was used.

Chapter 3
MEDIEVAL TIMES (1200S TO 1400S).

The Lincoln Population were still mostly living in the "Old walled area" developed by the Romans, although activities were beginning to develop to the East of the City.

Back in the Bailgate Area a construction, thought at one time to be of Roman times, was being built for improving the water supply in the area. About 14 yards from the present Assembly Rooms, a large excavation was made, 18 feet in diameter, dug completely circular to a depth of over 50 feet, tapering as it deepened and walled from floor to the surface. It was known as the "Blind Well" and maybe it did produce water, though it seems more likely it only stored it, as it was felt if this was a water source, how had the Romans overlooked it so readily, when just a few yards away in St Paul's Church yard, the Romans had dug a well in the centre of their market square. The "Blind Well" remained into the 1700s, it was then partly filled in and in the 1800s fully filled in and sealed off.

The religious houses arrived and this was the next significant change to water supplies in the City. The Black and Grey Friars or Monks were clever in engineering and architecture, and after establishing an Abbey in Monks Road to the East of the City and a Church in Broadgate (Grey Friars), they laid a lead pipe between the two. At the Abbey (known then as the Monks House), there was a Natural spring, (a chalybeate spring, the water of which was noted as a remedy for sore eyes and other ailments. Many years later in Victorian Times (1850s) it became a much visited Spa and was noted as equally as important as Tunbridge Wells. (This area is known today as Spa Street). The Broadgate church, was outside the City Gate.

Off Broadgate, close to St Swithins Square, they built a stone pillar and basin and installed the pipe outlet (Lincoln's first tap was born). A drinking water fountain had been made, approx 1/2 mile from its source. Some means of pumping must have been used at the source to create a water lift, as the ground levels were similar. Many Hydraulic pumping systems were known to be in existence, with probably animals being the driving force.

This water pipeline was to be extended many times, and in fact serve many rolls in its very long life. This sort of drinking fountain arrangement, later became known as a Conduit, although it was most unlike it's namesake back in Roman times.

Chapter 4
THE MIDDLE AGES (1500S ONWARDS)

The pipeline was extended via High Bridge down the High Street to St Mary Le Wigford Church. The council (who had, after the reformation taken control of the water system) bought 2 conduits from elsewhere and installed them on the pipeline. One outside St Mary Le Wigford Church, later called The Goodly Conduit, (although long since ceasing to supply water, it can be seen today), this Conduit was to supply the rapidly expanding High St for close on 400 years. Up to 1830 alongside this conduit were two recumbent effigies of Ranulphus Kime a wealthy merchant and his wife, these were taken down and put in the church yard, maybe they still exist?

This illustration shows water being drawn from the tap, looking closely on the wall above the man and little girl is one of the stone Effigy's.

The second conduit was installed alongside the Guildhall (this one supplied water until around 1730). This area of the City (High St) was becoming, by now, the trading area and so these water conduits would have been most welcome and refreshing addition.

The Goodly Conduit at St Mary Le Wigford Church*

To Fetch a Pail of Water

To get some idea of the water supply around this time, we need to look back at how the City was developing. This illustration shows the rectangular area of the "Old Roman City", to the North Newport developing along the Ermine Street, to the East was Monk's Lane with the Monk's development at Monk's Leys and Monk's Liberty.

This water supply pipeline ran from the Monk's House to Wigford on the High Street.

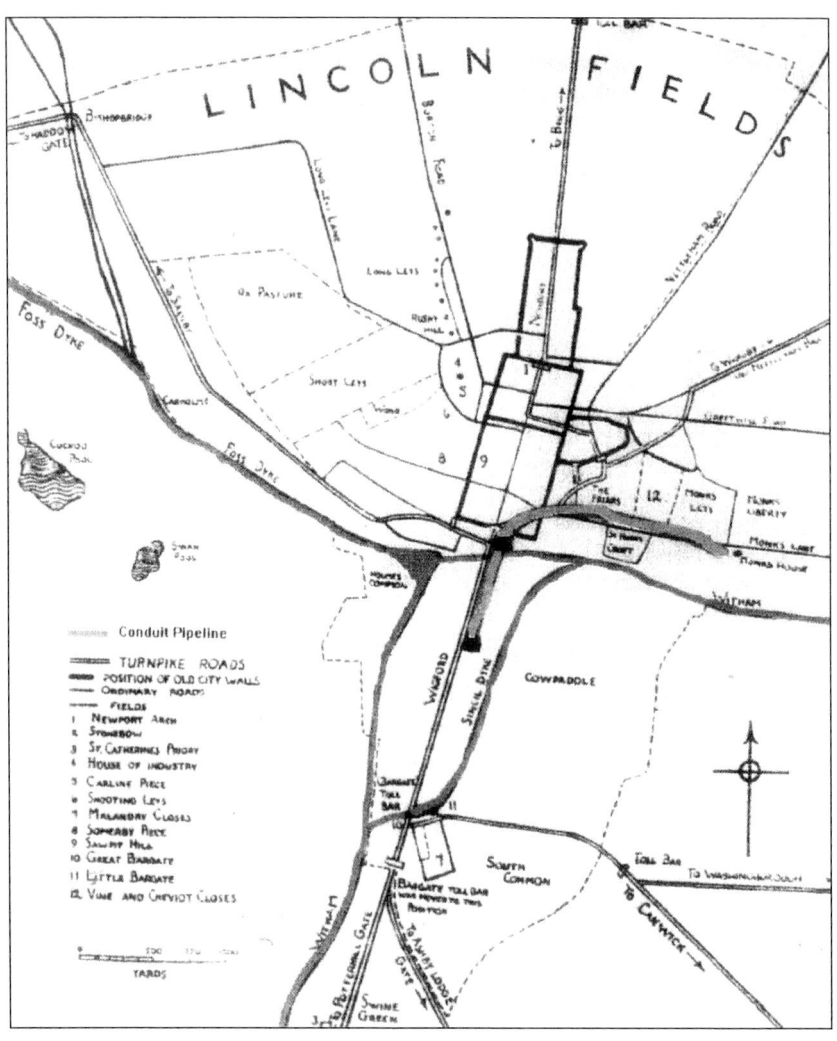

The spring water over the years had been occasionally contaminated and interrupted, but in general the conduits had been a source of reasonable water.

In 1571 a notice warned that
"Before Sunday Next!
All Sinkers* would be reformed!
and any found after then,
would Fine the owner
40 Shillings (40 /-) (£2 as today's equivalent.)
and Pain of Imprisonment
for 4 Days and 4 Nights

*Sinkers: from where waste water could flow into a watercourse, from kitchens, stables swinesties and fishmongers. ("Stinkers" would maybe have been a more apt name).

Clearly there was some means of monitoring the water quality and making laws to enforce them. Were these then (the Council) the first Water undertakers of the City.

Notices appeared again on 23 November 1595.
"No clothes to be washed at the conduits on pain of 5 Shillings (5/-)"
(25p as today's equivalent) and again on 5th September 1605
"No dust to be cast or swept within 6 yards of either of the Conduits on pain of 6 Shillings and 8 Pence 6 / 8 d" (33p as today)

The indications are that many more notices appeared over the years in the battle to keep the water quality safe.

The two conduits, along with the many wells, served the City for the next 100 years, and, as will be seen later, had a vital role to play some 300 years later.

Chapter 5
A WATERWORKS CHARTER FOR THE CITY

Described by The Gazette.
"GRANT OF CHARTER TO LINCOLN, January 1st 1695 The New Charter which His Majesty hath been graciously pleased to grant unto this City, having been sent by the Right Honourable the Earl of Lindsey, our Recorder, who is at present indisposed, to Sir Thomas Hussey; it was this day brought hither by him, accompanied by several of the Deputy Lieutenants and other Gentlemen of Quality who were met at St. Catherines without the City gate, by the Mayor, Aldermen and Common Council men in their Formalities and by about 3,000 of the inhabitants of this City and Liberties thereof; and from thence they proceeded to the Town Hall, the Trained Bands being in Arms and drawn up on both sides of the Streets through which they passed, the Bells ringing, Musick playing, and the people expressing their satisfaction with repeated Acclamations. Being come to the Hall, the Charter was read by the Town Clerk, and the Mayor, Aldermen and Sheriffs, where they drank the King's Health at the first Conduit which ran with Claret Wine from one o'clock till six at night, and the Gentlemen were entertained by Mr. Mayor at a very Noble Dinner; after which they all drank the Duke's Health at the other Conduit, which likewise ran with Claret Wine during the said time; the whole concluding with Bonfires and ringing of bells."

This Waterworks Charter for Lincoln contained many grants:
One being a fair should run the 2nd week in April each year, it should last for 4 days, 3 days for horses and the 4th day for all manner of things. (Was this the start of Lincoln's April Pleasure Fair? I believe it was). Also it was granted that there be a new Market every Tuesday throughout the year. This market was at a low level below The High Bridge.(was this when a market day was established).This Charter is today kept at the Guildhall.

The water works part of the charter granted for water systems to be kept pure and maintained and for clearing and maintaining navigational systems.

Corporation Manuscript 1727
"A treat to be given on October 11th for the Coronation of King George 2nd, the upper and lower Conduits would flow with red wine, for the Corporation to drink and a Hogshead of Ale for the Common folk to enjoy"

So the Conduits were to get a new lease of life, more were purchased and installed, design a conduit seemed to be the order of the day, the Guildhall conduit was removed and a further one, The Obelisk, was erected on High

Bridge after a Chapel was demolished in 1730. This was the regular market and trading area by now, so the Obelisk was a welcome addition, to the water supply system. The Obelisk was further restored 100+ years later and became known as the Albert Fountain, it was dismantled in 1939, so a very long life lay ahead. It has been restored again and now stands in the St Marks Shopping Centre, though only as a monument depicting its past and not supplying water.

These conduits were the water source for many years, for the lower parts of the City.

This was all very well for the lower part of the city, but the uphill part was still carrying on with the wells, though these were a little easier now with most having pumps fitted.

Lincoln High Street around the turn of the 18th Century, with the Obelisk standing in pride of place overseeing the proceedings of the tented market and the lower level market, below the High Bridge.

To Fetch a Pail of Water

Like the commonly used 3 feet (almost 1 metre) diameter vertical wheel, borehole pump spun by the rim (illustration 1).

Or the 2 throw pump wheel, (illustration 2) fitted with a handle at each side. This enabled 1 or 2 persons to operate it, allowing a faster rotation and therefor producing a bigger lift or pressure of water.

Larger water users were going for horizontal wheels fitted to 3 throw pumps, this allowed animals to be the motive power, the beast treading a circular path as it turned the large diameter wheel. The more beasts that were added the more the water and pressure increased, though a large turning circle area was needed for these pumps.

The main difference with pumps over the years was the motive power, man, animal, air, fast flowing water and wind (as illustration 3), but now rapidly emerging was probably the most powerful of them all, the awesome power of Steam.

Uphill continued with the wells, where many were being fitted with pumps or hand wheels.

Although in 1846 the city's water Source was to change dramatically, the spring supply from Monks Rd with its pipeline was to continue for reasons best known to the Council, for there didn't seem to be a need now, but thank goodness it did continue, as will be seen as this story unfolds.

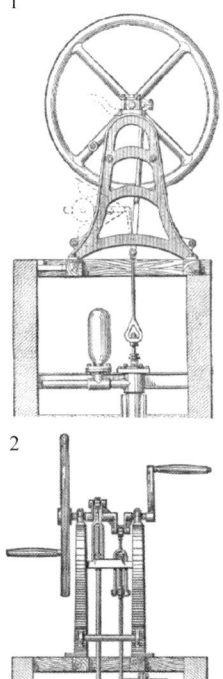

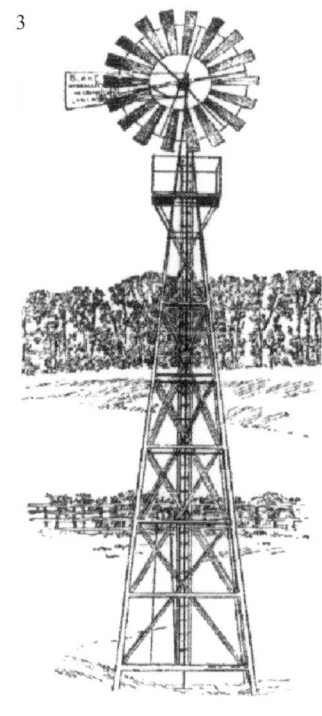

To Fetch a Pail of Water

Lets just continue with the conduit story! The number of conduits were to increase over the next Century, using the same supply from Monks Rd, even though a new supply was feeding the City, but, as mentioned in an earlier chapter, the water was supposed to be a good treatment for soothing sore eyes etc. the Victorians always enjoying their spa waters.

The pipeline was extended down the High St to St Peter at Gowts a conduit was installed and water was flowing from here in 1860.

Another Conduit of note was on Baggholme Rd, (as this illustration) it was connected to the spring supply in 1869. (this was only dismantled in 1968 to make way for a road alteration).

A further and final extension of the supply was carried out in 1890, this time the material was all lead. Lead was being used throughout the country by now for small pipes and connections for larger pipes or "Mains", made of cast iron. The lead pipe extending and terminating in Bracebridge, at a Horse Trough.

This Trough was of lead construction, perhaps the first time lead was used in Lincoln for holding a large volume of water.

The trough was presented to the City by the Rev C C Elisam and bearing the words "Peace, truth and Mercy" it was opened in October 1890.This trough was a well known landmark at the entrance to Brant Rd in Bracebridge, and I suspect the horses used by traders coming into the City here found it a very welcome stop.

This trough was dismantled only recently, after its comparatively short life.

Chapter 6
THE WATER UNDERTAKING OF THE CITY OF LINCOLN

On the 26th June 1846 an Act of Parliament was passed, quote from the Gazette, "for better supplying with water the Inhabitants of the City of Lincoln and certain parishes and places adjacent thereto in the County of Lincoln", and continued, "It was stated in the Preamble that the inhabitants had had an inadequate supply of water, and a constant, sufficient supply of wholesome water would be of great advantage, it is also ascertained that such a supply could be obtained and several persons, at their own expense, could make and maintain all the works for affording such a supply."

So with shareholders money and the borrowing of £6000 the Lincoln Waterworks Company was formed, some directors including the Mayor R Carline, were Mr S Leslie Melville, Mr G E B Padley, Mr R J Ward, Mr C Brook, Mr R Whitton, Mr F Andrew, Mr J S Battle and Mr Pratt.

The Capital of the Company was £18,000 divided into 720 shares, no one person should hold more that 40. Nine directors each must hold at least 8 shares of £25. A clause for the Limitation of profits to 10%, but with a provision of forming a Contingency fund. Also included was the greatest amount of any call on the shareholders should be £5 per share.

The act laid down the purpose of the company. To supply water, To make Reservoirs, Aqueducts and Conduits and the laying of pipes. The company was empowered to break up Streets for the laying of pipes, to use, divert certain springs and to divert the course of the Prial Drain and other water sources as required. And every engine erected for pumping water would have it's smoke consumed as much as was practical. "It was enacted that no service pipe should be greater than 1/2 inch without consent of the company. Supplies for domestic purposes would cost £6-10-0d per £100 of the Rack Rent or Value of the premises, per annum, or 1 shilling and 2 pence (1/2d) or 6.5 p in the £". Rented properties had a shilling (1/-) or 5p per £ added for the privilege. Fire plugs in the mains were to be installed at the expense of the City of Lincoln Commissioners, supplying the plugs with sufficient water was made the company's responsibility and no water charge for discharge from these plugs would be made.

The company would be penalized for failing to supply water other than Frost or unavoidable accident. (the same as today). Similarly the company could penalize any misuse or fouling of the water system. (were these then the first water bylaws?), taking water without consent, (were these the first licences?),

To Fetch a Pail of Water

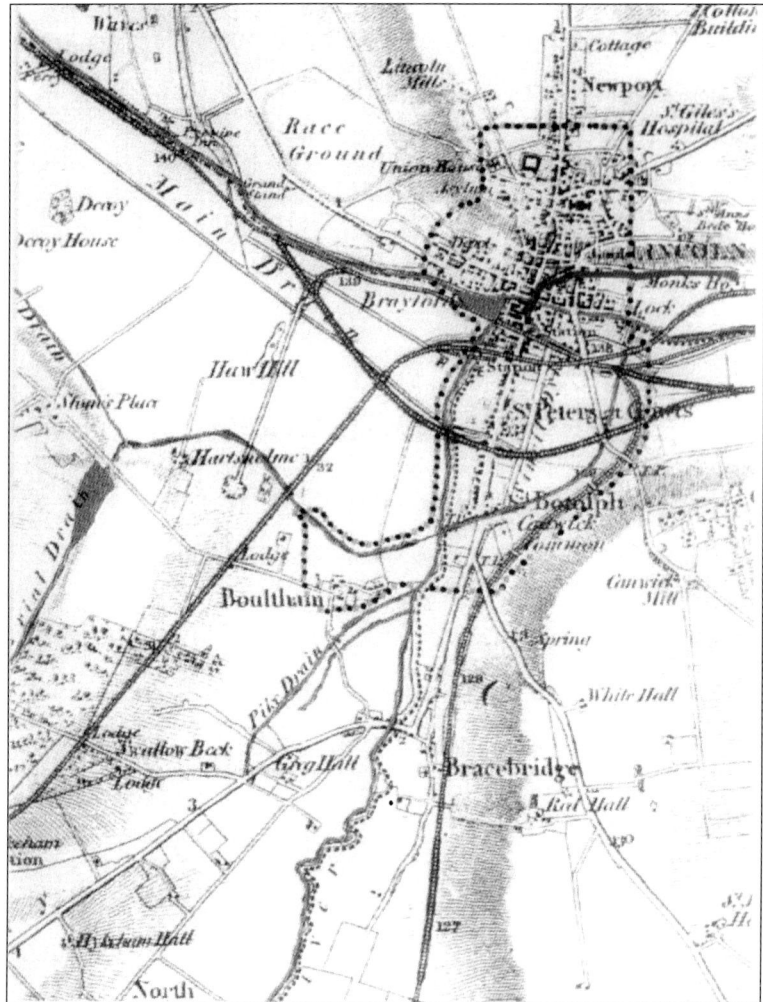

How it looked in 1846, the dotted section was the expected area of water supply and the line was the existing conduits supply

and suffering the apparatus through which water was supplied (again were these the first by laws?).

The area of the Company's supply was The City of Lincoln. The Castle, the Castle Dykeings. The Bail and the Close in parts of Lindsey and Boultham, Bracebridge, Skellingthorpe and in parts of Kesteven all in the County of Lincoln.

The area covered some 17 and 3/4 square miles. The secretary of the company was Richd Carline Esq, Chas Marshall was the manager and Henry Teague was the engineer.

To Fetch a Pail of Water

Upon the passing of the Act, works were put in hand and in 1848 by the damning of the Prial Drain an impounding Reservoir was formed in Skellingthorpe Valley (Hartsholme Lake). The Dam today supports Skellingthorpe Road, between The Hartsholme and Birchwood Housing Estates.

Hartsholme Hall with its lake, formed by the damming of the Prial Drain. From here a canal was cut some 2.5 miles long to within striding distance of the River Witham at Altham Terrace in Boultham. (This can be followed today flowing under Skellingthorpe Rd, Tritton Rd Boultham Park Rd and Hall Dr). The reservoir covered some 23 acres and had a capacity of 40 million gallons.*

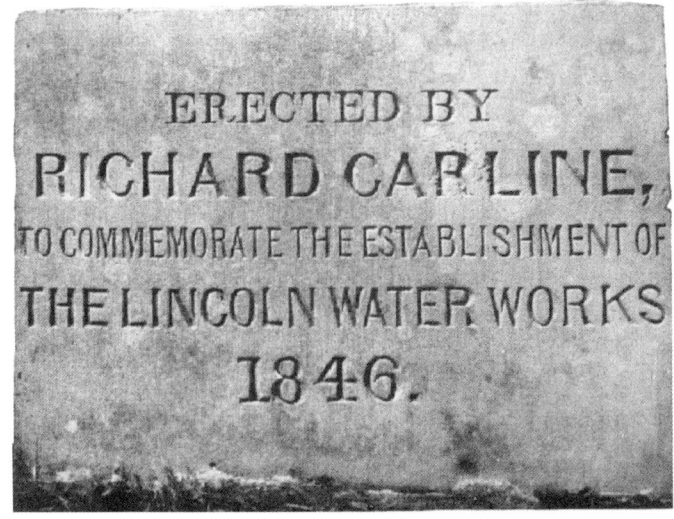

The engraving on the base of the column, in Hartsholme Park.

To Fetch a Pail of Water

The Hall was demolished some years ago, but the lake is today much as it was 150 years earlier. (photographed from a similar angle, recently).*

A view of the Reservoir from the Hartsholme side, on the right is the dam and the outlet sluice releasing water to the Boultham Works. Looking over the water, almost in the centre, is a column erected to commemorate the establishment of The Lincoln Water Works.*

To Fetch a Pail of Water

At Boultham, 2 sand filters were constructed 572 square yards in total, these were slow sand filters used for treating the water to a drinkable standard, (much like the one in the photograph below). Water arrived at Boultham via the open canal from Hartshlome Reservoir.

Slow sand filter

Also an engine house and attendants cottages with other associated buildings, were built here. (This area later became the Boultham open air swimming baths, the pump house and cottages remained until well into the 1980s)

A 9 inch Cast Iron pipe was laid from Altham Terrace to Westgate, where a service reservoir, with an open top, was constructed (it is thought on the same site as the Roman Reservoir, many centuries earlier), its capacity was 777,000 gallons. The main delivered water into the reservoir over a standpipe, with a non return valve fitted in the main as it reached the hill top, this was to prevent water flowing back down the hill from the Reservoir when, in times of high demand, water failed to make the hill top. A 6 horsepower gas engine was fitted at the Reservoir to draw water out of the reservoir, over the standpipe to supply the remaining uphill section of the City.

A pump, driven by a 33 horsepower steam engine, was installed at Boultham, the unit was purchased second hand from a Cornish tin mine. It was a 2 cylinder compound engine, the space between the 2 pistons being at all times open to the condenser, the cylinders were 25 and 50 inches diameter with a stroke of 8 feet. The plunger pump was 12 inches diameter and was fitted to the other end of the

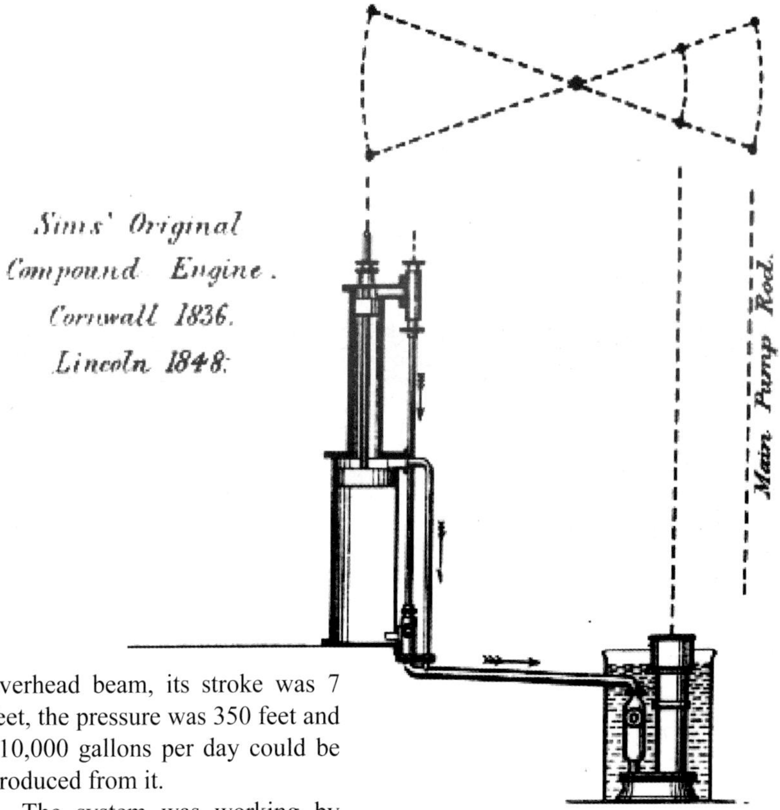

Sims' Original Compound Engine.
Cornwall 1836.
Lincoln 1848.

overhead beam, its stroke was 7 feet, the pressure was 350 feet and 110,000 gallons per day could be produced from it.

The system was working by 1849, with some 733 houses being supplied, the City population being about 17,500. Mr Henry Teague had achieved something that had never been done before, that of Water being pumped to the uphill parts of the City from a downhill source.

Though Lincoln once had pumped water uphill, it had taken 1300 years to get back to to where the Romans had begun.

Lincoln's Water system had finally caught up with the Romans!

The First pump at Boultham

To Fetch a Pail of Water

A popular method was to install a standpipe in a backyard of a terrace block, this way many houses would have access to water. (as seen here)

The backyard fire hydrant/water tap

Or the backyard stand pipe/tap

To Fetch a Pail of Water

Over the next 50 years the City's population was to increase dramatically, as industries began to arrive. Was it the more reliable water supply that attracted the Industrialists?

Certainly the Industries came, Clayton and Shuttleworth, Robey and Foster, Dawson Leather Belting Works, Poppletons Sweet Factory, Cannons Glue Factory, Ruston and Lincoln's largest Ruston and Proctor.

During this time the demand for water was also to increase dramatically, Boultham was to increase its pumping to an engine size of 40 horsepower, this pump was a single cylinder with a double acting flywheel engine with a combined piston and plunger.

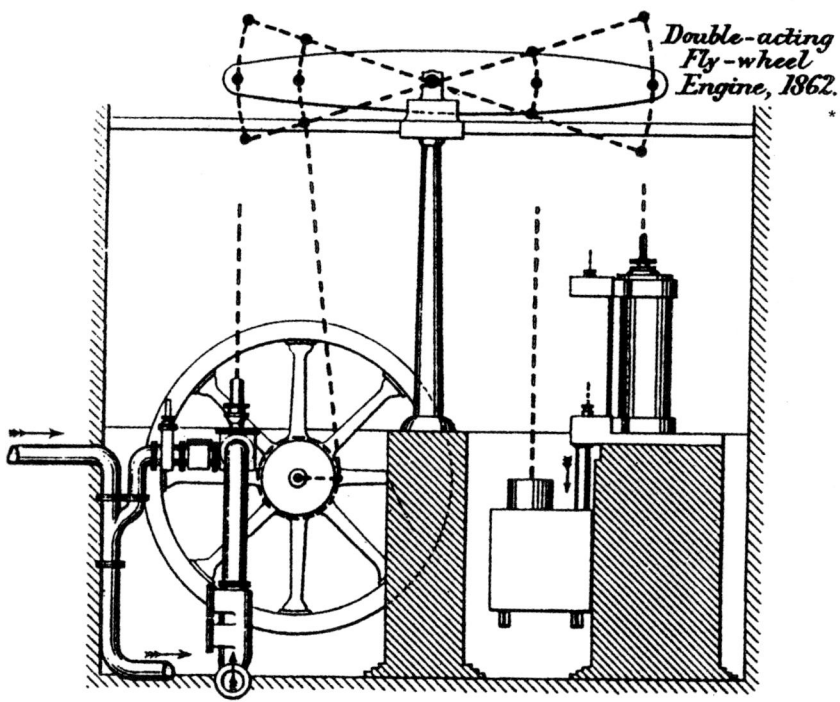

A book published in 1861 called The Strangers guide Through Lincoln. Quoted "The beautiful shaft of the engine, of the Waterworks Company, is seen in the fields to the right after passing St Botolph Church. The water is obtained from the Prial Brook at Skellingthorpe where an immense reservoir has been formed".

A Map Of Lincoln City mid 1800s
The round mark indicating Boultham Works and the dotted line indicating the large mains feeding the 2 reservoirs at uphill Lincoln and Bracebridge Heath and the thick line showing the extended conduit pipeline.

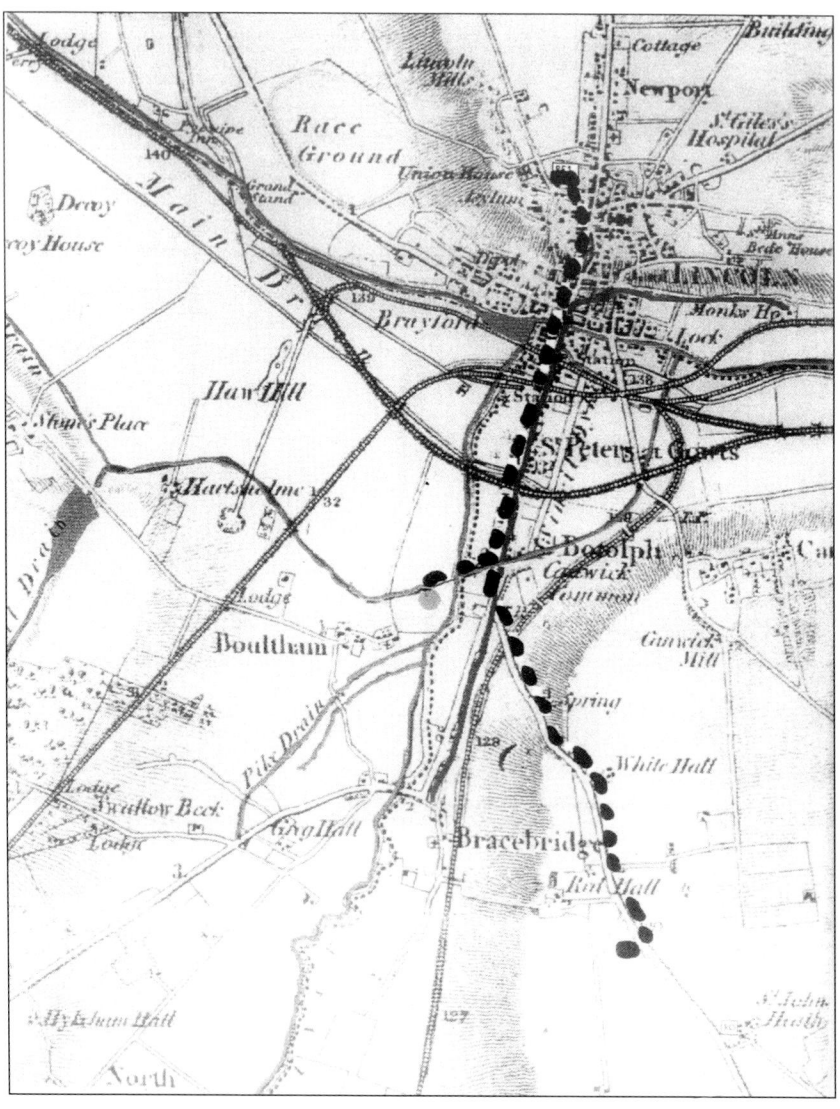

Chapter 7
THE SANITATION METHOD

As with all life forms we eat, we drink and we produce waste, the more we consume the more waste we make. At this stage then let's take a glimpse at what was happening on the waste or sewage side of things.

The practice had for many years been the chamber pot, (the potty or poe or the many other slang terms used for this simple bowl), its contents were cast into the garden cess pool or even onto the garden, similarly waste water would be cast to any handy drain, stream or the cess pool!

The more up market people, would have a piped waste and drain, from an inside bowl in a small room (the water closet). These bowls had seats and an overhead tank, after use a handle would be pulled, this would lift the plug/valve in the outlet hole at the bottom of the tank and release the water, the full contents of the tank, emptying or flushing into the bowl. (not much different to today's system, you may say). On releasing the handle, the plug/valve would drop back in place and the tank would refill, ready for the next flush, the tanks had a ball cock that would shut off the water when full.

A lot of these systems, though, would have the handle tied down, so the water could flow continuously into the bowl and in turn continually flowing into the cess pool below, this was a way to keep the bowl clean at all times, wasteful maybe, but effective none the less.

For the ordinary folk, though, it was a totally different story! The Chamber Pot was probably a luxury, a bucket or a bowl or even a hole dug in the ground with a wooden seat on it, outside somewhere, would be nearer the truth.

The houses being built at this time were changing though, there was now emerging a new room, the Privvy! (known to many as the Thunder Box), this was built, usually in brick, in the back garden and it was simply a private room that had a pot or bucket, with a seat, the bucket would be emptied regularly onto the garden.

The outside toilet. Dark, cold and often visited by other than humans (vermin)

The garden waste caused all manor of devices to be used to make more tolerable the area. Even under the Privvy seat ashes from the coal fire, hot coal/coke clinkers, lime, and even fires would be started to clear the area. Another option was a horse and cart. (The Dilly Cart), would call weekly to allow people to dispose of their waste, the attendant would ring a bell to warn of its arrival, although I guess you may have known of its arrival long before you heard the bell.

How much would it cost to empty a pot? What wages would the attendant get? I wonder?

Next on the scene came the Septic Tanks and the Cess Pits, these could store and to some extent control the waste, smells and gases. Dug and built in a large hole in the garden then covered and ventilated, with all the waste from the house being piped into them and with an access hatch being fitted, for emptying to take place as required, all making a very tidy and hygienic system.

At least that was the idea!

To Fetch a Pail of Water

The expense of emptying cess pits was not however popular, to empty a cess pit could cost the equivalent of a weeks pay! So not many got emptied! A popular trick was to fit an overflow, to allow discharge of the liquid into the garden or local drains.

The illustration exaggerates, but shows how waste was handled and allowed to flow into a water course. I seem to remember something called a sinker in the 1600s doing a similar job! The council imposed fines and prison sentences then! Had the standards changed?

The plumbing trade had for some time been a highly dangerous job, as most of their calls would be blockages in the sewage system and the gases that were generated from these were highly flammable and stinking. Most of the areas they worked were dark, and they had nothing in those days to illuminate the area, other than a naked light, so I guess it was a choice, work in the dark and risk getting soaked after un blocking the system! be gassed! or light a candle and be blown up.

To Fetch a Pail of Water

Reducing the amount of flushing caused more blockages, so more work for the plumber; the increase in flushing caused fuller cess pits, so more emptying was required; either way it was expensive.

It was around this time a device, invented by Thomas Crapper, came along, this was to revolutionize the whole of the sanitation and plumbing system. The syphonic flushing Water Closet or valveless water waste preventer was made available, the Crapper Cistern was fitted to a Twyford toilet closet in a Royal Palace and so this was it, the ultimate unit of the time. The wealthy wanted to get something close to this and were rapidly having the system installed, alongside the basin, the bath, and now a water closet with flushing water at the pull of a chain.

The need for water increased as more of these systems were installed, with 2 gallons (9 litres) required per flush and many flushes per day were possible. So the flushing toilet cistern had arrived and a very clean and efficient method of discharging all the waste in the bowl was established, it was to become the largest user of water in the domestic world. Very little has changed to the flushing W.C of today, or indeed the 2 gallons (9 litres) still required to carry out this, many times daily, deed.

Chapter 8
HOW QUICKLY THINGS CHANGE

Lincoln had developed into a busy little industrial City, housing was developing off the High St and further South into Bracebridge.

In 1871 a further act of Parliament and this allowed the handing over of the Water Company to the Lincoln Corporation. The Corporation paid £59-18-0 for every £25 share held and paid off outstanding loans, the total cost being £63,837, a price fixed by arbitration. By this act the limits of the supply were extended to include Canwick and Greetwell. Also a sewage works and waste disposal works, along with a combined sewer and drain system, were to be built.

The first engineer, for the Corporation, was J H Teague, taking over from his father Henry Teague who had been the Water Company's brilliant engineer of the past 25 years. The system needed extending and the first move was to build a further Open reservoir, this time at the top of Cross O Cliff Hill, opposite the Lunatic Asylum (known more recently as St John's Mental Hospital), the capacity of this Reservoir was 1,200,000 gallons. The water mains were also extended into Bracebridge, which had now become part of the City.

At Boultham ballast pit water was used to further support supplies and another filter was installed. By 1875 the River Witham, downstream of Bracebridge, was opened to the Works, to use as req'd, as a final support for the ever increasing demand for water. Was this cocktail, to be the start of a tragic mistake?

Although by 1880, a large Sewerage network was in place, taking surface and sewage water from the City, to a works at Great Northern Terrace and a farm at Canwick, Bracebridge had not been connected and so the practice of allowing overflows to discharge into the nearest water course was allowed to continue here and as all water courses would eventually find their way into the River Witham, then the new intake at Boultham Works, was, surely, infected!

The Bracebridge area of Lincoln continued to develop, as did the water mains system, but not the sewers. Notices sent out by the Medical Officer of Health to the Lincoln Corporation in 1879, 1883 and again in 1885, were mostly calling attention to the use of "night soil" and town refuse as manure on the light sandy soils that formed the water gathering grounds to the South of the City and it should be noted that this could have an affect on the water supplied to the City.

The Corporation responded by advising that it was a well known fact, country wide, that 1 in 3000 were dying of typhoid and many others of cholera and although these were highly infectious diseases, the cause was not necessarily caused by polluted water supplies. What was not mentioned, or possibly

To Fetch a Pail of Water

This photo shows the covered headwork's with the borings scattered and steam escaping from the engine area. To the left of the ladder, through the gap can be seen the terraced housing alongside the River Witham.

ignored, was that the cause of these diseases were most certainly poor sanitation.

Were the people being Hoodwinked? This was the opinion of some at the time.

As demand continued to increase the practice was to take more water from the River Witham. A further pump was installed at Boultham, this one, driven by a single acting Cornish engine whose cylinder diameter was 58 inches with a stroke of 9.5 feet and a plunger with a diameter of 18 inches its stroke being 8 feet; it was capable of moving 2,000,000 gallons of water a day, to support the needs of a population nearing 37,500 and the increasing industrial needs.

This illustration, shows the working drill at Boultham.

In 1891 a special committee of the corporation was formed to check out the water supply system in the City. It concluded, after an intensive investigation, that the water was safe and a fair second class supply! and considering the cost of a new source it was satisfactory and should continue.

In 1901, it was decided more water was needed, this time below ground was thought to be a more reliable option and below Boultham Works was the most likely and convenient area to produce a large quantity. So boring was started with the hope of a 1 million gallon a day yield from the Red Sandstone below and a loan of £24,000 was taken for this work.

The boring continued at a snails pace for the next 5 years, drill failures and lack of know how by the contractors being the main excuses.

Chapter 9
THE DARKEST DAYS

Lincoln's population had increased to around 50,000, by 1901, the water system had continued to extend to meet the ever increasing demand, yet more filters were added at Boultham, 2,000,000 gallons a day could be produced and was during the summer of 1902 and again in 1904. The end of November 1904 and 2 cases of typhoid were reported! This was not classed as unusual by "those who should know", was the response, "after all 25 had died in 1879 without a deal of concern and on average 2 were dying per year of the highly infectious disease".

In December of 1904, 10 cases of typhoid fever and by January 10th 1905 18 cases, the Medical Officer of Health reported to the Corporation a serious outbreak was here and a Public Notice should be issued, warning of precautions to be taken! The Corporation declined! The reason? To avoid a panic. Lincoln Corporation finally issued Boiling Water Notices on January 21st 1905, "2 weeks too late", some said, but issued only in the Sincil Drain area where most cases were occurring, 15 minute boiling notices. (It was thought 15 minutes was the time required to rid the water of disease). Could anyone in this area afford to do this? Most men would earn up to a £1-0-0d a week, skilled maybe as high as £2-0-0d, a harsh winter was already taking its toll, on money and fuel.

Lincoln's Typhoid epidemic struck with such speed and startling suddenness, that by February 4th there were 408 cases and 23 deaths. The Corporation, although acknowledging the need to boil water, maintained that a dry summer followed by a cold winter, had drawn water through the Boultham filter beds too quickly and polluted it and with an extra-ordinary high rate of burst pipes, caused by harsh frosts, the pollution had increased as output had increased. They claimed, also, that medical measures they had taken were proving effective in the fight against typhoid.

This announcement was quickly proved wrong, by February 21st, 61 people had died and 732 were now suffering from the disease.

The people now became afraid and turned away from the water on tap and went back to the wells used 50 years earlier and the old conduits that had continued in use from the medieval spring on Monks Rd, though the spring water had been condemned with the water deemed unfit to drink, non the less a crucial and vital role it played in the months ahead as the people drew from these daily. A spring on Yarbourough Road also played a part and proved popular at the time.

To Fetch a Pail of Water

Water was brought in by railway tankers from Newark, as above. Others waited in various prearranged areas in the City for the horse drawn water carts to arrive below.

To Fetch a Pail of Water

Many visited the conduits, like this one on Baggeholme Road, to get their daily requirements. With the policeman, no doubt, helping in this hour of need.

Others waited as shop keepers gave water free in large bowsers like below. Other shop keepers would buy water from a spring at Welton and sell it at 1d a bucket.

To Fetch a Pail of Water

Sadly also was the sight of the horse drawn ambulance, arriving at Chaplin Street Chapel or the Drill Hall on Broadgate, where temporary hospitals had been set up for sufferers of typhoid all being cared for by nurses of the Bromhead nursing staff.

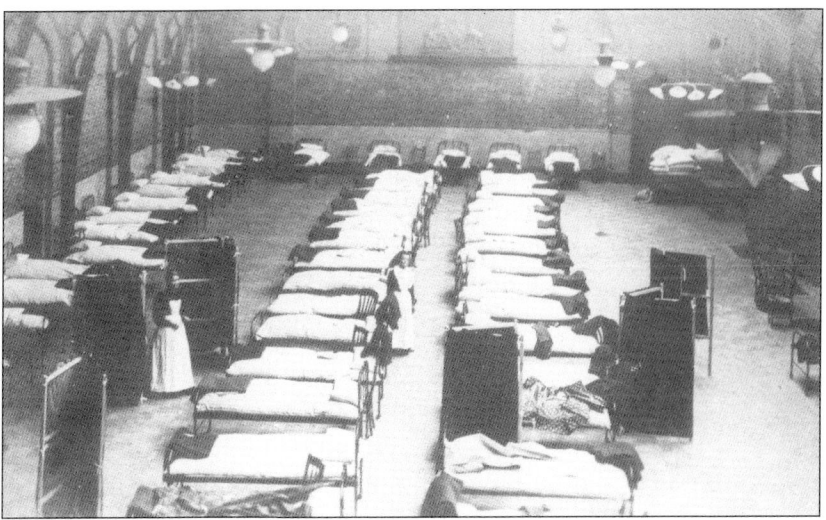

To Fetch a Pail of Water

The mood of Lincoln people and visitors to the City, was of fear and suspicion. Train passengers, passing through Lincoln closed the carriage windows and held handkerchiefs to their noses, while the trains were in the City limits.

A well known baker and confectioner, (Henry Kirke White) put a notice in his High Street shop window:-

**"Corporation water is NOT used in our
tea rooms, only spring water
obtained from the Conduits!".**

Amongst the dead by now were Mr W H Curtis, the corporation sanitary inspector and the head of the "mineral water manufacturing company", in St Rumbold Street.

The Spring Horse Racing meeting on the Carholme in March 1905 produced the smallest attendance ever recorded. Those that did arrive brought their own food and drink, and left the City afterwards. The Great Northern Railway announced that their normal passenger load was down by 7000 and the Hoteliers in Lincoln had a disastrous time.

By April 1905, 1,006 people had the disease and 113 people had died, but the notifications had started to slow, typhoid was no longer at epidemic level.The Lincoln Corporation supplies were now tasting horrible after the introduction of Hypochlorite of Soda (the taste being that of Chlorine, the first time it had been used in this way in the country). The public for their part, put a piece of sulphur in the water to try to make it more tolerable. ("A bucket full of daisies", was the term used then, for this effect).

The Great Northern Railway continued it's generous offer of bringing water daily, into the City by tanker, Willoughby and Newark was the supplier. The daily routine of waiting for water to arrive and using any vessel to carry it in, continued.

The worst was over and by the 12th May the final tally was reported as 1045 infected with 131 dead. Of the 12,277 houses within the City, patients had been treated in 8,190 of them.

Had one of Lincoln's darkest hour's finally come to an end?

Chapter 10
A CITY ON THE BRINK OF DISASTER

Five months the City had suffered illness, trade had slumped, the people were shattered, no one had confidence in the water and the Corporation were in a state of chaos, with a large problem to solve and quickly. The London Press made the most of it, by embarrassing all and making out Lincoln was an undesirable place to visit, with a daily blow by blow account of the City's water problems.

What could the next move be?

The Corporation started by shutting the intakes from the Pike and Catchwater drains and The River Witham (this later was to resume upstream, at a point outside the City). The Engineer in charge resigned (maybe he was pushed!), few it seems were held responsible for the tragedy, but also, it seems, the villain of the piece was not proved either,

Was it the water? Which water? River, Drain, Pits....? Or was it the treatment or lack of it?

A new engineer was appointed and this little known engineer, Neil McKechnie Barron was to become, "the man of the moment", he had an enormous task to tackle, possibly his biggest was to regain the confidence of the people to the water supply, his name, eventually was to echo through the water engineering records of Lincoln City forever!

Mr Barron or McBarron (as he became known) quickly moved to improve the filters at Boultham and have one last try at the Borehole, now 2,200 feet deep and the deepest well in Britain. Water eventually flowed, the volume was as expected, but it was found to be salty, and declared unfit for human consumption, so £24,000 and five years had been wasted, a further embarrassment.

Where now?

Clearly a new source was required! Many were offered, Newark, Manton, Tealby, Bourne, Sleaford and The South Lincs Water Company, a committee was set up to investigate the future supply and the cost.

Meanwhile, under the control of Mr Barron, the Hartsholme Reservoir outlet and the Ballast Pit supply were fitted with Cast Iron pipes feeding Boultham and the open canal shut off in an attempt to prevent any further contamination.

The Boultham Filters were brought up to standard, a long overdue requirement. Automatic recording of the filtration rate and filter bed resistance, were installed, from now on the whole operation, for the first time, was to be conducted and operated on scientific lines.

To Fetch a Pail of Water

This is a slow sand filter in use today, it has a similarity to the Boultham Filters used many years ago

A new aeration tank and clear water reservoir were constructed. (This part later became the first of two open air swimming baths of Boultham).

1905 had not quite finished with it's extremes though, a dry summer caused drought, drinking water became scarce, Hartsholme Res level dropped to its lowest level on record, the River Witham was low and many nights were spent trying to increase the flow into the Water Works at Boultham.

This was Mr Barron's first taste of Lincoln's plight, I wonder if it crossed his mind, to pack in there and then, while he was still accepted in the City. Well thankfully, even if he had had this thought, he did not show it and decided to carry on.

Horse drawn water carts, (at a cost of £160 a week to the council) were on the scene again, with the people again waiting in the streets to fill their pales. Thankfully this time though because water was scarce and not polluted!

This didn't stop the London Press, they could have a go at the City's appalling water problems, once again. Why? 1905 had been such a tragic year for the Lincoln people, surely, the worst was over now, so why inflict more sorrow and embarrassment on its people.

By 1906 Lincoln's water supplies had been put back on the road to recovery, the River Witham was supplying Boultham again, but only at times when water levels permitted, and from a point farther upstream of the City, out of harms way and from any pollution.

Bracebridge was now connected to the main sewers, but the general view of most, was still of suspicion and distrust, the old conduits were, as far as the Lincoln people were concerned, still the only trusted drinking water on tap in the City.

To Fetch a Pail of Water

Mr Barron advised that although the City was receiving a water supply, it wasn't adequate and its quality was unstable! A new source should be found and a new system should be constructed as quickly as possible. The debates went on, the arguments raged, the planning faltered, the costs? Well of course the root of most of it was the cost!

Mr Barron reported in 1907 that wherever the new source, Lincoln required a covered Reservoir; as an open reservoir, likened to those in the City at present, caused great deterioration in the quality and purity of the water. This Reservoir should hold 3 days of supply of water for the City. Also a Water Tower should be built in the uphill area of the City, as pressure was inadequate here. To complete the scheme there should be 2 new rising mains one to each site and linking, via the High Street, to each other. The cost of this scheme was £50,000.

One person much respected in the community, as he was throughout the tragic times of the Typhoid epidemic, was Bishop E King. He worked with the Corporation and McBarron he argued about the City's water supply system, trying to convince Lincoln Corporation that a new way should be sought and that Mr Barron should be given more support in his efforts to achieve this. He also talked to the people of the City many times to calm their doubting thoughts, he listened to them and spoke on their behalf. His efforts alone possibly set the Corporation in a new direction, the costs were still important, but now the new supply was the main objective and funds would be made available to get it. The first signs of their change of direction was a grant of the £50,000 required to build a Water Tower and Reservoir.

Something different, but very special to the people of Lincoln and a surprise to the persons concerned, happened. Above is a photograph of a Silver Medal struck by J. S. Ruston, which is on display at the Usher Art Gallery, this and similar medals were awarded to nurses for their services rendered to the sick and dying, during the Typhoid epidemic a year ago.

Chapter 11
A WATER TOWER FOR THE CITY

A Water Tower was to be built next to the open top reservoir close to Reservoir Street, in Wickham Gardens on Westgate. The design was to be of the highest quality and eminent architects were asked to tender their designs, Mr Barron submitted his own as a water engineer of the highest order, though his and many others were to give way to the Reginald Blomfield's design.

The building commenced in 1907, with the West facing wall strictly parallel with the Cathedral West facing wall and thereto all the structure being square with the Cathedral.

The Water Tower rising from its massive foundations

The tower was seen gradually rising from its massive foundations. The inner being circular brickwork, the outer being square in plan, of local stone. The design is very heavy and substantial, the quoins and bottom portions being tooled stonework, having the panels filled in with rock-faced rubble, the contractors were Henson and Son of Wellingborough.

Being 56 feet square outside with a 48 ft. 9 ins. inside diameter at ground level and 117 feet 6 inches high to the top of the parapet wall. The circular brickwork supporting the tank is 4 ft. 3 ins. thick, the outer stone being parallel and supporting the roof to the tower.

The tank is 52 feet in diameter and of mild steel plates throughout, their thickness varying from 5/16ins at the top to 1/2 ins at the bottom, it has a hemi-spherical bottom, all riveted together. The contractors for the tank were Newton Chambers and Co Ltd,of Sheffield. The top water level is 330 feet above ordnance datum, 117 feet above ground. The vertical sides are 17 feet 6 ins. deep and terminate in a compression member from which is hung the spherical bottom, having a radius of 34 feet. The depth of the tank in the centre is 31 feet and the holding capacity is 300,000 gallons, (1,356,000 litres) representing about a day's supply for the uphill district.

The weight of the tank (when full of water) is over 1,400 tonnes, the weight is taken by the compression member, a built-up girder, 2 ft. 8 ins. deep by 13 3/8 ins. wide. this rests on cheese-shaped rollers which in turn rest on a cast-iron bedplate 18 inches wide, set on stone templates on the top of the brickwork.

Five pipes pass through the bottom of the tank namely, three 20 inch diameter, one 12 inch and one 6 inch, a stuffing box and gland being provided in each to allow for any upward and downward movement of the tank.

Underneath the bottom of the tank is a moveable gantry, one end carried on a circular rail on the brickwork and the other on a centre platform or crow's nest supported by the three upstand pipes. This gantry may be revolved from the centre platform so that any portion of the tank bottom can be inspected or painted.

A spiral staircase is provided in one of the arises (corners), for access to the roof and tank and a winch is provided at tank level for the hoisting of material.

The inlet pipe (1st of the 3, 20 inch pipes) passes up to the top of the tank and down again to the bottom of the tank, to ensure complete circulation of the water and to maintain a uniform head on the feed pumps. A twelve inch outlet pipe, fitted with a reflux valve (a valve to prevent return flow), goes from the bottom of the tank into the main to supply the uphill district when pumping ceases.

The 2nd of the 3, 20 inch pipes, passes to within 80% of the top of the tank, where an open belmouth is fitted. This pipe, then, drops to ground level and on into Lincoln High Street and on to link with the inlet of the new reservoir.

The 3rd of the 3, 20 inch pipes, passes to the top of the tank, where a belmouth is fitted. This pipe dropping to ground level, leads to the open reservoir, (still in use at that time) in Wickham Gardens and acts as an overflow.

The construction of the Water Tower underway

To Fetch a Pail of Water

The Tower complete, notice the open top Reservoir still in use during construction.

The Water Tower today taken from a similar position to the photo of 1911

Chapter 12
A RESERVOIR FOR QUALITY AND SECURITY.

Whilst the Tower was being constructed, much was being debated as to the position of the new Reservoir. The old Reservoir, opposite St John's Mental Hospital on Cross O Cliff Hill, as we knew it, was not in a desirable position and ground conditions were far from ideal. McBarron insisted on a larger area where the rock formation was reasonably close to the surface, this area was in Bracebridge Heath, but some several hundred yards further South. The Corporation, advised by their Engineer, acquired land on Grantham Road in the Village of Bracebridge Heath, as this was thought to be the ideal position.

Work started in late 1907 and was to continue for 5 years.

The picture shows some of the early tasks in building the Reservoir.

To Fetch a Pail of Water

Below the round structure taking shape, the track in the foreground carried the steam crane back and forward, it was capable of lifting items into or out of the reservoir.

The Reservoir was circular in plan and the main wall was of mass concrete, with a vertical outer face and a battered water face, having a radius of 131 feet 9 inches measured to the outer face. It is 9ft thick at foundation level, 3 feet thick at the top and 22 feet high.

A further view showing the circular form with the finished inner wall taking shape.

The floor is laid on the solid Limestone and is 12 inches thick. The roof is 7 inches thick reinforced with expanded metal and is supported by mild steel arched channels and rolled steel joists carried on columns of rolled steel joists

Picture showing inside the construction with the columns and joists.

on end and riveted together, secured to padstones embedded in the concrete floor. The column joists are encased in concrete and the exterior finished circular and rendered.

The reservoir was lined throughout with Asphalt and a feature of the reservoir construction was that the wall and floor were built in 8 separate sections to allow for contraction or expansion during construction.

Below with the columns and joists in place, whilst running across the centre of the reservoir is a division wall 10 feet high to facilitate cleaning without putting the reservoir out of use.

The floor of each half of storage area falls to a channel running along the centre wall to a sump where the bell mouths of the scour and delivery pipes are fixed, these pass through the wall to the vault where all the control valves are situated.

To Fetch a Pail of Water

Over this vault is built a Valve House of brick, faced with Ancaster Stone with an approach stairway to the Reservoir. Above the Valve House is a small elevated tank, for the purpose of supplying Bracebridge Heath Village dwellings and Waddington Aerodrome, developing a mile or so South of the Reservoir.

Access to the Reservoir was via the Valve House, built on top the Reservoir, stepping down a stair case of concrete, the sides of which were dressed with white glazed tiles. The staircase splitting into 2 directions for easy access to each half of the Reservoir. White glazed tiles surround the floor area, as the channel, the outlet and the scour are all situated here.

To Fetch a Pail of Water

All the water flowing into the reservoir, from the City / Westgate main, would push into the high level bell mouth and fall into an elevated tank, holding 1000 gallons. The water would overflow from the tank and run into 8 inlet points at the circumference and centre of the reservoir, this was to assist circulation of the water as it entered the reservoir, before it flows through 2 outlet pipes, one from each half of the reservoir. These 2 outlet pipes then couple together within the valve house to form one main, this laid alongside the incoming main back down Cross O Cliff Hill to couple up to the mains at the foot of the Hill.

The Reservoir's top water level is 252.5 feet above Ordnance Datum (sea level), 19 feet 6 inches above the Limestone base, this was 40 feet,(12 metres), above the ground level of Westgate Tower it was to hold 6,000,000 gallons of water, which was 3 days of supply for the City.

Almost ready to go the valve house, entrance hall and water tower overlooking the giant reservoir.

Chapter 13
A NEW SOURCE IS BORN

By 1907 the construction of both storage sites was well underway and now the new source was the priority. Surface or near surface water in or near Lincoln had been ruled out, on grounds of indifferent quality or insufficient quantity.

The South Lincs Water Company were back vigorously pressing their offer, which was 6% per year of their capital layout and the cost of pumping to Lincoln, the Corporation rejected this, mainly on the grounds that they wanted to be masters of their own water supply and who could blame them for that, after all they had been through in the past 3 years and the bad press they had suffered Nation-wide. The Water company continued to press their offer, why pay more when a plentiful supply at Bourne was available, they were to cause quite a stir during the tricky months ahead.

Mr Barron had been overseeing most of these alternatives, whilst working on a scheme of his own to which he submitted a report, in fact he presented 13 extensively detailed reports, detailing each option available. He put each scheme's points and considered them against 9 Key factors, Not too hard causing high costs for softening, Good quality and costs for filtering, Quantity with costs of pumping, Location with cost of pipe laying, Reliability of quality and quantity and the Time it would take to install the scheme.

It was agreed that water below ground was the only reliable option. The schemes submitted, included the Boultham bore (it had cost a lot of money already and maybe there was still a chance of salvaging some water), various combinations of blending it were considered, with Hartsholme Lake, the Ballast Pits and / or the River Witham as the main options.

Schemes from Newark, from Willoughby, from Newton on Trent (Red Sandstone), from the North Lincs Limestone (Welton, Dunholme Area), from Potterhanworth, from Metheringham. from Dorrington, from the estate of the Duke of Newcastle at Manton Colliery in Notts (only ruled out on a possible pollution problem from the mine), and finally from further into Nottinghamshire beyond Manton Colliery (the outcrop pebblebeds of red sandstone).

Eventually down to just two schemes, Dorrington from the Lincs Limestone, or the Notts Red Sandstone. The scheme Mr Barron had submitted, the Notts Red Sandstone, finally clinched it, the costs were classed as reasonable considering the short time involved implementing it (3 years) and unlike Dorrington no softening would be required, it was felt the rate payers would not want to bare the high annual costs for softening.

The red sandstone at Boultham possibly inspired his idea, as it was this outcrop he pursued to its shallower level, the Pebble Beds of red sand (The Bunter Sandstone) were tracked into Nottinghamshire and were, already, being used by the City of Nottingham, Retford Town, Mansfield and Newark.

"The Bunter", was an immense underground source of water, it spread from Nottingham, in the South, to Bawtry in the North, some 40 miles across, with an area of 200 square miles. Water was within 30 feet of the surface and close to 600 feet deep, so abundant was the water that it was estimated, if after 3 dry years, 30,000,000 gallons (140,000,000 litres) could be abstracted per day without causing harm or recordable losses in levels! So Lincoln's requirement of 2,000,000 gallons per day would not be classed as a threat, although many didn't see it that way and objections were raised at the very idea! "Poachers!", was one phrase being used at the time, because of the objections the whole scheme was to go to the courts and eventually to the House Of Lords, for a decision.

Mr Barron's recommendation was to abstract water at a place 22 miles from Lincoln, 5 miles from Retford, 3 miles from the Checkerhouse Railway Station on the Great Central Railway and 1 mile from the Great North Road (A1) in Sherwood Forest of Notts, at a Village called Elkesley. The scheme would take 3 years and with the tower and reservoir due for completion by then, all would come together and the City would have a new water supply by late 1911 and at a total estimated cost of £248,000, it seemed very reasonable and it got the Lincoln Corporation's full support, all it needed now was the official approval.

A difficult passage, through the courts and government, lay ahead, with objections from Notts County Council, should water go from one county to another? With Mansfield, Sutton-in Ashfield, Retford Council, Lord Belper and several other land owners, mostly objecting to the poaching that could cause a threat to local supplies. The South Linc's Water Company were back and they made a strong case for Lincoln to have for their own County Supplies.

For the Corporation side there was Mr Barron, the Deputy Town Clerk Mr Page, F.H.Livens and C.W Pennell, they took up the fight, with others giving support.

The Elkesley to Lincoln Water Bill finally got the Royal Assent on August 11th, 1908, although, it seems, a bad feeling was left between those involved.

So Lincoln was to get its long awaited water supply, but the Bill laid down certain conditions, the limits of the supply were to be extended to include Saxilby with Ingleby, Hardwick, Burton, Broxholme, Riseholme, Cherry Willingham, Reepham, North and South Hykeham, Mere, Heighington, Washingborough, Branston and Waddington: The Corporation were also placed under an obligation to afford supplies in bulk, if called upon to do so, over an area of some 120 square miles of Nottinghamshire, this was all a concern, the system would need to be made bigger than planned, was this unknown extra load to become a burden in the years ahead?

To Fetch a Pail of Water

After finalising the negotiations of acquiring the land from the Duke of Newcastle, this being on hold until the Bill was passed, the next step was the test pumping for quantity of water at Elkesley, this was the critical and most important part of the whole scheme, before any contract was let, the yield or reliable quantity of the source had to be proven.

October 24th 1908 some 50 Lincolnians travelled the 22 miles, in 16 cars, to a clover field in Nottinghamshire, close to the village of Elkesley.

Here the first sod was to be cut to mark the drilling point for the first borehole. A silver spade was specially made for this purpose and it sits today in Lincoln's Guildhall. Bishop E King invoked the divine blessing and the Mayor, Councillor J H Mills, turned the first sod and as if rehearsed, the heavens opened and down poured the rain, so they all retreated to the nearest pub, the Hop Pole at Ollerton, to continue their Agenda.

Outside The Hop Pole at Ollerton, with the spade that started it all.

This first hole was drilled to a depth of 570 feet, within 30 feet of the base of the pebble beds and for 22 days test pumping was carried out non stop, these were anxious days, could the bore sustain an even flow without reducing others? The bucket of the pump was 300 feet from the surface, the natural rest level was 30 feet and the draw down of level, at 1,500,000 gallons per day, was 81 feet, this was better than expected and well within the requirements; so the first obstacle was passed and the way ahead was now clear for stage two, the quality of the water.

It was decided, after some early samples had proved favourable, to start the scheme, as it was most important that a supply of water, from the new source, should be available at the earliest possible moment. To sink 4 boreholes in the first instance and add wells, with additions, later if necessary, the contract was let to A C Potter and Co of London.

January 3rd 1909 the first borehole was started, 36 inches diameter at the top with 3 reductions in diameter as it deepened to the base where the diameter was 20 inches. Lap welded tubes, grouted, lined the top 170 feet, it was then unlined to its base of 587 feet. By April 30th all was satisfactory with quality, many samples had been sent to London over the 4 months, and the water was found to be of the highest quality.

No2 borehole commenced on June 20, No3 commenced on July 30th and No4 by Aug 16th, all 4 being identical and completed, by the end of September. Again samples of water for each and any combination of bores were tested and approved as a very high standard.

Activities at Elkesley could now get into top gear, Ashton Frost and Co of Blackburn, were contractors for the pumping plant and Wm Crane Ltd,of Nottingham were the contractors for the site and buildings.

The water flows from Number One Borehole.

Chapter 14
THE LIFE LINE TO THE CITY

With the source secured the main laying part of the scheme could now get underway, the contractors for this were Bower Bros of West Bridgeford Notts. The main was to be laid, for a few miles, by the side of the Great North Road (the A1 as we know it now) and then all the way to Lincoln by the side of the A57. The pipe was 21 inches in diameter and was to extend for 22 Miles, it was of cast iron material; apart from railways and river crossings, where it was of lap-welded steel. The contracts for the supply of Cast Iron pipes were offered to two different companies, The Stanton Ironworks Company of Nottingham and The Staveley Coal and Iron Company of Chesterfield, with all valves and fittings to be supplied by Blakeborough Bros Hydraulic Engineering Co of Brighouse, Notts.

The River Trent was ideally placed, in one respect, as barges could be used to bring a lot of pipes from their makers to the centre of the system, so too was the Fossedyke Canal, the railways transported others and horse and cart did the rest. Cranes, driven by steam (on the right of the above picture) were to be seen at all the delivery points, as a single pipe would weigh close to one and a half tons.

To Fetch a Pail of Water

On October 7th 1909 the Mayor, Councillor W.S.White, carried out the laying of the first pipe of the Elkesley to Lincoln Trunk Main. Such was his enthusiasm that he insisted on operating the chain pulley himself and lowering the pipe into the trench. The site chosen for this first pipe was Burton Lane End, adjacent to the A57 (Lincoln to Saxilby Road), the mayor was presented with a keep sake, of a small scale of the pipe and so commenced this arduous task laying the main over 22 Miles.

Mr Barron, along with 3 assisting engineers, as with all the scheme so far, had designed, planned, tested and inspected everything, the pipes were to be no exception! Each pipe would be numbered, after inspection at the factory, a log of each pipe on delivery would be made, its number and its location. Each joint (with run lead poured onto a single lead band, with one pipe slotting into another) would be tested and recorded with its own unique reference. The pipe was also classified as to its strength, this was done basically on wall thickness, Class J or even K were not unusual, with wall thickness' of up to 1 and 1/8 inches being common place, no chances were being taken!

The pipes arriving by barge on the River Trent close to the Toll Bridge.

Above the registering of the pipes. This was Mc Barron's way!

Transporting of the pipes.

Bridging the River Trent was a separate contract and carried out by the Cleveland Bridge and Engineering Company. The bridge was constructed alongside the toll bridge and had sufficient width for a second line of pipes if necessary. It was built of steel, with 6 spans, 1 of 262 ft, and 5 of 66 ft, a total of 592 ft. The steel pipes laid over the bridge were lap welded tubes, with riveted reinforcing bands and bolted flanged joints. An interesting feature here was on the Notts side, the main dives beneath the drains and streams causing 2 by 90 degree bends to bring it onto the bridge, but on the Lincoln side the main goes over the washland on concrete stilts, giving a slower curve for the main, this was a requirement of the agreement, Notts C.C. did not wish to see any of the pipes on the Notts side of the River Trent.

Also a meter was fitted on the Lincoln side to record the water transferring from another County and people from Notts could check that Lincoln was taking only its authorised share, (if you remember this was one of the great obstacles in the Water Act hearing). The recorder for this was to be accessible and here a brick building was built to house it and because the lower part of the building was below the River Trent flood level, so the recorder had to be put at a high level inside.

The Cleveland Company was also to construct the pipe over the Roman Fossedyke Canal at Saxilby. Curved mild steel pipes ¾ of an inch thick, with bolted flanged joints, and an air release valve situated at the highest point. With a platform and railing leading to the valve for safe access during maintenance. This pipe is self supporting, concrete abutments with ashlar stone facings are built each side of the canal acting as both anchors and thrust blocks. Spanning some 79 feet the pipe has a radius of 51 feet with a rise of 16 feet.

Another view of the pipe over the Canal in 1911

To Fetch a Pail of Water

The scene at Saxilby as the huge trunk main makes its way to Lincoln.

The 22 mile of pipe laying was underway at a good pace, many contractors were employed at various locations along the route. The weight of the materials, the deep trench digging, the timber trench support, the man handling with ropes and pulleys, (bear in mind, not much in the way of machinery had been invented at this time), a cart, carrying 2 pipes pulled by 2 horses, needed guiding on the long walk, (could be 5 to 6 miles), to their workplace, this all added to their arduous working day, starting at daylight and finishing at dusk.

Unforeseen difficulties were to add to their task, a heavy snow covered winter, making the walk difficult and, at times, preventing some getting to work at all. They also came across a bog 3 miles beyond Dunham village Notts side, it was half a mile long and 20 feet deep. It was necessary to drive in piles into the more solid earth below and lay the main on them, a set back overcome.

The route of the main from Nottinghamshire to Lincoln City.

64

To Fetch a Pail of Water

The pipe crossing the River Till at Odder.

The story would not be complete without some account of the investigations that lead to a bitter fight in the law courts. Suspicion fell on the Staveley Company over the marking of the pipes and somehow many were slipping through without inspection. The contract was thrown into question and accusations were made, a good many pipes were in question! The Company retaliated by suing the Corporation for fulfilment of the contract and damages!

A long and bitter fight was expected! In fact, by the time it got to court, it lasted just 7 days. The Corporation's suspicions were found to be true, they received not only costs, but also substantial damages. The Company, although failing their case, were found to be unknowing of the fraudulent tinkering of others within and were therefore found Not Guilty of other accusations.

The pipeline laying continued, ground levels varied as it wondered its way toward Lincoln and air release valves were fitted at each high point, these can still be seen today, in tact and in use. Another fitting used, in various places, was a non return valve, fitted in the pipeline to prevent the pipeline water draining back, so when the pumps were stopped supplies could be maintained along the system. These valves were substantial and they each had four cantilever flaps, each flap weighing hundreds of pounds and made of solid brass, these flaps would close shut if the flow in the main stopped.

An Air Release Valve as the main rises from Elkesley.

Back in Lincoln, meanwhile, a healthier water was being sent to the public main from Boultham, it was not plentiful, it was warm and tasting earthy, though it did seem to be tolerated, maybe because the new supply was soon to be arriving.

The streets were being ripped up, Union Rd, Spring Hill, Grantham St, Broadgate, Kesteven St, Sincil Bank, onto the South Common sweeping round to the bottom of Cross o Cliff Hill and up to Bracebridge Heath; the City trunk main, varying in diameter from 21" to 18" and all the distribution pipes, to serve the people with the new water, were being laid. The Contract for this was in the hands of R C Brebner of Edinburgh, made of cast iron the trunk main was to be the artery of the City's Water System, linking the up hill and downhill supplies.

Connecting Westgate Tower to Bracebridge Reservoir and to the High Street mains, meant the Lincoln Gap had been crossed for the first time, water pressure supporting high level plumbing systems throughout the City.

To Fetch a Pail of Water

The dramatic scene in Lincoln in 1909 as the water mains system gets a major overhaul.

Chapter 15
THE HEART AND LIFE BLOOD.

This was already an engineering scheme second to no other in the country, but the master piece was still developing in the depths of Nottinghamshire and Sherwood Forest. Designed, planned and engineered by Mr Barron, the heart of the scheme was emerging. Messrs Ashton Frost and Co, Ltd, were to design and build the pumping system.

Using the nearby Checkerhouse railway station and siding, with an extended track built to the lower level of the Elkesley site, for the delivery of the materials with the contractors themselves setting up living accommodation on site at Elkesley, for a long stay lay ahead.

The 4 boreholes were situated in a square, 36 feet apart and 570 feet deep. Suspended in each bore, at 314 feet below the engine room, were the deep well pump's buckets and clacks, the buckets being 18 inches in diameter, with a stroke of 5 feet, were to be driven from overhung cranks. The buckets and clacks were of the accordion pyramidal valve type and the pump rods were 11 inches square of pitch pine.

The scene at Elkesley, with 3 boreholes visible.

These pumps were to raise the water to the surface, through condensers, passing into a semi circular settling tank, where the redsand fell out of suspension, allowing the cleaner water to pass to the next stage.

To Fetch a Pail of Water

From this tank the water flowed over a weir into a suction pipe, common to the triple plunger high lift pumps which would dispatch water to Lincoln. The high lift pumps were housed below the engine house with rams, of 16 inches diameter, driven by side rods forged to the piston rod crossheads above, the pumps with air vessels stood some 25 feet high and 15 feet in length, the air vessels would also take up the shock of water surge when the pumps were started or stopped.

The High Lift Pumps.

Built above all of this was to be the engines and if the pumps were to deliver millions of gallons a day over 22 miles to a high level in Lincoln, then they needed to be substantial in every way. It had been decided from the start that two engines would be required to power the works, one to run and the second to be in standby mode, ready to take over in the event of any failure. The engines would be run on alternate weeks to each other, so as to age them equally and allow maintenance work after each week of pumping.

An early showing of the engine

To Fetch a Pail of Water

Each engine would drive two deep well pumps and the high lift pumps and therefore creating a lift of water from the underground depths of Elkesley to the highest levels of Lincoln City with a single rotation of the drive shaft.

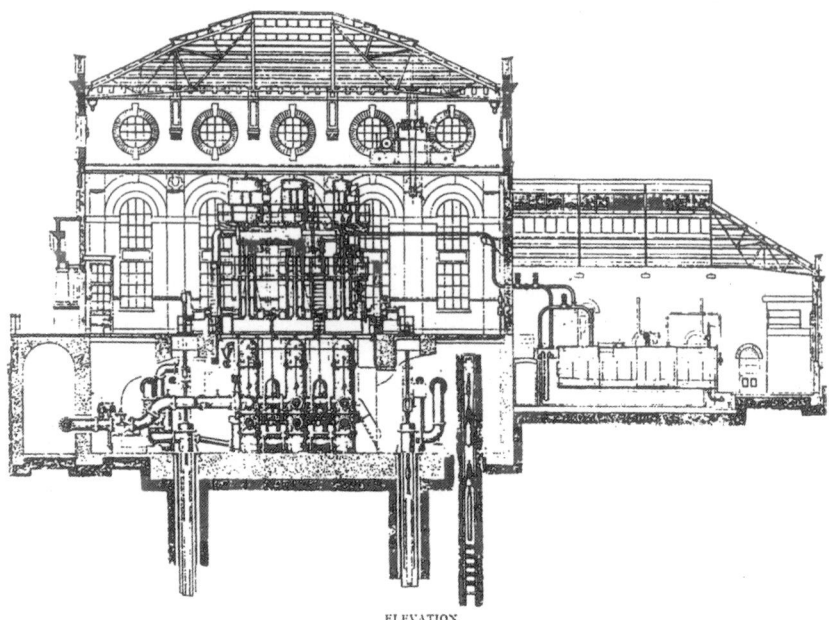

ELEVATION.

The above shows the original design and layout drawing of Elkesley, the Engines above the high lift pumps with the deep well pumps suspended at each end. To the right is the boiler house.

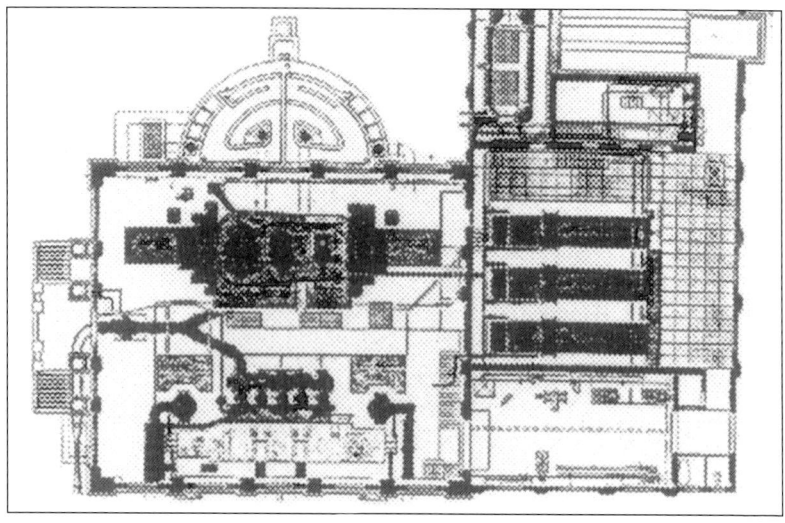

Plan

To Fetch a Pail of Water

The Power House one of the 500hp steam engines

Substantial engines are what the site received, 2 triple expansion inverted direct acting rotary steam engines. 500 break horse power, each weighing 250 Tons and standing 25 feet high with a length of 36 feet. Each engine having 2 fly wheels with a diameter of 17 feet each weighing in at 17 Tons.

The steam engine's 3 cylinders were 26 ins, 45 ins and 68 ins in diameter each weighing over 4 tons, with a 4 foot stroke and with cranks at 120 degrees to each other, the sequence being high, low and intermediate. Corliss valves were fitted for the inlet and exhaust to each cylinder, with a cut off being fitted to the high pressure cylinder, controlled by a governor, the other 2 cylinders were to be adjusted by hand whilst the engine was running.

Each cylinder would have a steam jacket on the end, as well as its barrel and receiver, fitted between the cylinders and fitted with reheat tubes through which steam passes.

The high pressure governor

The condenser had a cooling surface of 780 sq.ft and was placed in the delivery pipe of one of the deep well pumps. The air pump was of the Edwards type and driven direct from a bracket on the crosshead of the high lift pump adjacent to the low pressure cylinder. The two fly wheels on each engine were situated at the end of the bedplate and between the neck and the over hung crank.

The already extended railway track sweeping down to the lower part of the site, was extended further to the engine house, here a large steam crane was erected to assist in the installation.

Steam for operating the engines was to be supplied by three Lancashire boilers. The boilers, supplied by Ruston and Proctor of Lincoln, were 28 feet long with a diameter of 7 feet, with two internal flues.

Designed to a working pressure of 180 psi, fitted with Ferguson down take type superheaters, arranged at the back of the boiler, delivering the steam to the engine at about 540 degrees Fahrenheit.

The hot flue gases, after leaving the boiler, pass to a Greens economiser before, finally, passing to the chimney, a filter for the feed water was also provided.

The Ruston and Proctor boilers producing the steam for the engines, complete with the stoker and another operator of the works.

As the engines and boilers were most important, many years of service were hoped, so the building housing them would have the same consideration.

A ceremony, carried out by the Mayor Councillor C.T.Parker, to lay the foundation stone of the building, was attended by the Town Clerk, the water works committee, other councillors, Mr Barron, Bishop E King and the contractors. The commodious building was constructed of brick with terra-cotta

Above the gathering after laying the commemorative stone at Elkesley, with the Mayor CT Parker holding the trowel that started it all

facings, standing 58 feet high with an apexed raised roof, 75 feet long and 64 feet wide. with many large arched windows each having circular windows above, allowing maximum daylight to pass inside.

A twin staircase leading to a four pillow porch and twin doors, to be beautifully crowned with carvings and inscriptions, as this was to be the focal point and welcoming main entrance.

The original carved medallion laying claim to the prime position, depicting, on its left, a goddess like figure, ministering to a dying man, with the legend "1904", (the typhoid epidemic) and on its right an Arcadian allegory of health and happiness, (the new water), though it never got further than the planning committee, for it was thought that the subjects were too pointed, in that the new water was not forced out because of the typhoid epidemic, but because of the failure of the Boultham bore.

To Fetch a Pail of Water

The Stone Carving above the imposing entrance to the engine house

The carving that did get the crown position, was a delight, on its left a 1908 key stone being prepared by skilled people,to depict "The year of Salvation" and and on its right a block, engraved 1911 (the year of deliverance) with carved figures, depicting a scene of health and happiness, into the future and forever more.

Another carving, or several carvings as it were, was very prominent and totally encircling the outer engine house in between the arched and circular windows like a girdle, with the letters a foot high, was carved, in stone, a Latin inscription which read, "Aquae Purissimae Fons Jugis Civitatis Lincolniae Felicitate Munditiae Salubritate Dedicatus Anno Sautis MCMVIII".

Translated to read
"A fountain of the purest water dedicated to the health, cleanliness and happiness of the City of Lincoln, in the year of our salvation 1908".

On the front of the engine room an inscription simply read "Lincoln Corporation Waterworks", with the Lincoln City Crest carved between each word.

The main hall had the boiler house attached, with a height of 20 feet, with a width of 42 feet and a length of 55 feet it was again spacious and was built big enough to house

On the front of the engine room an inscription simply read "Lincoln Corporation Waterworks", with the Lincoln City Crest carved between each word.

a fourth boiler, it was felt a fourth boiler would be required in the future.

Additional buildings on site, were an engineers house, complete with committee room and a block of three cottages to house employees and their families, these were sited close to the boiler house.

The final piece to be built at Elkesley and towering majestically above the site, was the chimney, detached, but close to the boiler house. The chimney could be seen for miles around and was probably the only indication, to most, that this works existed. All the building works were carried out by Wm Crone Limited, of Nottingham.

The completed site, with the roadway entering from the left middle, sweeping passed the engineers house, through the Avenue of trees to open at the front of the engine house. A branch road to the back yard, where the large coal bunkers were housed. The main drive continued to the 3 workmen's cottages, then down to the red sand waste lagoons, at the bottom of the photo and finally leading to the lower forest and the river. The rest of the site was grassed with layered banks stepping down to the forest, all complementing the beautiful clearing set in Sherwood Forest.

In the forest, down hill of the site, another construction was completed, this was a sewage and waste water works. It treated all the waste from the site and dispatched the cleansed liquid to the river, running along the base of the site.

Chapter 16
A LITTLE TOUCH OF BRILLIANCE

The New Water was coming; the people of Lincoln were quietly expecting something special; industry waited in wilful anticipation and the Council hoping, this time, all would be well and confidence restored. Sadly Bishop E King would not see his tireless efforts come to a conclusion, for he died only months from its completion.

1911 and this was to be a year in Lincoln's History that was to change its way of life forever. The water tower had appeared on the sky line and stood majestically as the second highest structure in the City. The people had been kept informed of every event along the way and there was, surely, a hint of excitement in the City. The streets were getting back to normal, with all the mains and service laying coming to a conclusion.

The new Mayor of Lincoln, Councillor Clement H Newsum, along with the Town Clerk, Mr W T Page, were to have the pleasure of presenting the new water to the City, although the last three Mayors were not holding back with their continued enthusiasm for the scheme. October 3rd and 4th were the dates set for the official start up and the turn on of the new supply, a little quicker than the 3 years estimated at the start of the scheme.

July and tests were underway, the giant steam engines were rotating and the new water was arriving at the Westgate Tower. With 22 miles of mains being tested, the engines performance to be proved and the many fittings to be checked. Elkesley works would need workers to operate around the clock, stokers, engine drivers and boiler men, a superintendent and an engineer were also required, the interviews and appointments were well underway.

Much was still to be done, to fill the water main and the tank at the Tower, alone, it would take 2,000,000 gallons of water, this was a days supply of water for the City! Quality and clarity were to be checked, meticulously, with samples being dispatched to the Public Health Laboratories in Cambridge.

The water level in the tower was calculated by a vertical 6 inch pipe being installed alongside the 30 foot tank at Westgate, a small pipe connected to the tank allowed water to flow from the tank to the 6 inch pipe, the water level in the tank would then be repeated in the vertical pipe. A brass ball or float was then suspended in the 6 inch pipe going up and down as the water level in the tank fluctuated. Fastened to the float was a wire chain, run through a couple of pulleys to the base of the tower, here it linked to a cog wheel which drove a two handed clock mechanism, the clock face was calibrated in feet and inches, rather than hours and minutes, the small hand indicating feet and large hand inches, so an accurate water level was recorded at ground level.

The flow from the Tower was recorded locally, a venturi meter immersed in the outlet pipe, gave the information to drive a mechanical gearing system, this moved a pen up and down a calibrated chart, indicating flow in gallons. The chart was cylindrical and was rotated by clockwork, with one full turn representing a week. Several dials of varying amounts, from a single gallon to millions of gallons, were recorded from this mechanism, so as well as the weekly pen chart showing peak flows, a totaliser was also available, showing the total flow of water that had passed to the uphill part of the City from the Tower. A brass clock, its clockwork mechanism with a swinging pendulum all fully exposed, was installed to drive the flow recorder chart and covered with a glass cabinet, making this unit, as with so many items in this new water scheme, a delight to the eye and an easy system to Operate.

A similar flow recorder was fitted to the Elkesley discharge pipework, so the water usage could be determined from the source to the City and the amount discharging to the uphill, from the Tower.

The Reservoir was coming on at a fast pace, but it was not expected to be completed in time, in fact it wasn't due now until next spring. A flow recorder, similar to the others, was installed, this time though it was to record the flow out of the reservoir recording the flow to rest of the City system.

The water was flowing to Lincoln and beginning to flow into the public supplies, slowly but surely the" big day" was coming. The City people were getting an early sample of the new water. Quotes made at the time,

"**it looks so clean and tastes so good**", **Lincoln Leader**,
"**it tastes so cold and nice**", **Lincoln Gazette.**

Much was also being done in the Arboretum, this was to be the venue for the first sight of the new water and for celebrations after the turn on. A fitting and appropriate place in more ways than one, for it was the Monks pipeline along here which had brought water, for the first time, by pipeline to the Lower part of the City, way back in the 1400's. A fountain was being built here, with the first six cores of sandstone, drilled from each of the four bores at Elkesley, standing centre stage and supporting the main spout. This fountain minus its ornate top stands here today, it was built by a Lincoln stone mason J.W. Thimbleby.

A large platform was also being built alongside, this was to hold all the officials on the "big day" and to be the main stage for the big turn on. The preparations as to who to invite? What to organise? An evening banquet? and whether women should be invited? entertainment, who and what? many debates ensued, many ideas were posed, The Water Works Committee, of the Corporation, still had much to consider.

An interesting piece of News, in the Lincoln Chronicle, the headline read **"Mischievous Boys Break Insulators"**, the Water Works Committee including

To Fetch a Pail of Water

Mr Barron, some small boys from Saxilby and the Police were all involved?

What had happened was, the Police had caught some young boys, in Saxilby, throwing stones at the telephone poles, hitting and smashing the glass insulators. This was a dedicated telephone line installed, by the engineers, to carry communications between Lincoln and Elkesley and was vital to the running of the scheme. The Police asked if charges were to be made? Mr Barron pointed out that "since the line had been installed, some 350 insulators had been smashed and communication had been, at times, non existent", he added, "repairs had been costly and time consuming" ; but he felt the boys "had maybe learnt their lesson and should be released". This the Police did and, I guess, this was the last they heard of the problem.

These telephone lines, had another use as the system came more into operation, this was yet another piece of ingenuity, the level recorders at Westgate and eventually at the Reservoir were wired up to the lines, allowing information to be transmitted to Elkesley. At Elkesley a barrel chart with 2 pens similar to the flow recorder, was installed.

One pen for the Westgate level and the other for the Reservoir level, each time the water level changed by 6 inches, a pulse would be sent down the line and the pen at Elkesley would move 6 Inches. So a very effective level recording could be maintained at Elkesley and the Engines could be driven at a speed to maintain the desired level in the Tower or Reservoir at all times.

The Fountain at the Arboretum*

Chapter 17
THE CHRISTENING

Tuesday October 3rd 1911, all was ready, most invitations had gone to the notable citizens, the magistrates and the press, an open invitation had also been offered to all with an interest. This was to be the press day for Elkesley, a time for Lincoln Corporation to show off their new scheme, with a special message to the London and provincial press, a time to get back a little satisfaction and pride, after 6 years of bad feeling and harsh press coverage and a time to show the Country that Lincoln had not only recovered from the brink of disaster, but was back with a water scheme second to none in the Country.

Vehicles of all types, trains, bicycles, horses and carriages, even walkers, but mainly by, as the Mayor put it, "the luck of the motor car", converging from all directions, on Elkesley and locals from Nottinghamshire, particularly from Retford, were there. Some didn't make it from Lincoln in one go, due to brake downs on the way, or the" unlucky motor car", but all arrived eventually, albeit somewhat late.

At 1.15pm, in Lincoln many watched the cavalcade through the Streets, after the arrival at the Great Northern Railway Station of the VIP,s, as they were collected and escorted to the source 22 miles away, in cars labelled "Magistrates", "Press", and "Council", "a sight equal to any ever seen in the City".

At 3.00pm arrival at Elkesley, stepping into the main building they where met by others and some three to four hundred people were now gathered. One of the giant engines was slowly and quietly revolving, a pulse of moving machinery could be heard and a buzz of activity as people were admiring and photographing the engineering splendour of it all. Just before the entrance (outside) great interest was of looking down into the white tile lined duct, in which could be seen the crystal clear water making its way from the depths of the earth to the settling tank below the engine house.

On a platform, above one of the huge fly wheels, in the engine room, were the men who were to show and explain the scheme, the Mayor (Coun, C.H. Newsum), with Alderman Wyatt and City Member, Mr C.H.Roberts all to the fore, and, as described by, The Leader Newspaper, "to his side-in the fullest and plainest sense of the word-was the Waterworks Engineer, father, creator and perfecter of the scheme, Mr Neil McKechnie Barron, who may have been a proud man that day, but bore his honours modestly," and continued, "He was all simplicity, all anxiety to give every possible information, every disposition to make the event a people's show and discount himself."

The Mayor opened proceedings by expressing his great pleasure in welcoming the citizens and said "they had come to see that which was well worth seeing", and then handed over to Mr Barron to describe the machinery, a little cheer greeted him, a short speech and a loud applause followed. The Mayor then turned as if to walk away, seemingly forgetting the main reason for the visit, Mr Barron responded and returned to the rail and said "in order to have the books properly kept, the engines should, in true marine style, be named". (up to now they had been referred to as Gog, the one currently pumping and Magog, silent and cold by Gog,s side).

The Mayoress was found (she had stepped down), and brought to the fore where there was a large bottle of champagne (Cuvee Reservee1900 for the curious), hanging from a double rope from the roof, with a swing Mrs Newsum smashed the bottle against "Gog" and naming her "Janetta", after a little lady in her home, their daughter.

The Mayor then stepped forward and said he thought all would agree, nobody could be more suitable to christen the other engine than the engineer's wife, Mrs Barron, she duly stepped forward and after 3 attempts, (1 glanced off, the 2nd bounced off), the 3rd smashed against the cold engine of Magog, Mrs Barron then named it "Livens", in tribute to the service Councillor Livens had put into the water scheme.

It is thought many names had been discussed for the engines, "King" after the late Bishop, "Mc Barron" after the engineer, being 2 front runners.

Though some of the people of Nottinghamshire weren't having any of it, they had already Christened them "The Lincolnshire Poachers", this was alas to remain as a "Nick Name", for in their book, they believed the people of Lincoln were poaching their water.

A cheer, applause and an army of photographers then bombarded the area to end the proceedings and retire for afternoon tea, before all returning from whence they came, proud and well pleased with what they had seen, those from Lincoln were all safely back by 7.0 pm, "the luck of the motor car" had held.

To Fetch a Pail of Water

Gathered on the steps leading to the Steam Engines, the Lincoln Civic Party, the Waterworks Committee, Contractors and Engineers with Mr Barron (front row centre) flanked by his wife and the Mayoress.

Chapter 18
DELIVERANCE

Wednesday the 4th October 1911 had finally arrived, the Day of Deliverance. A special holiday and a highly emotional day, for most, lay ahead, many had lost loved ones or had suffered, only 6 years previous, during the typhoid epidemic, was this then to be their Salvation Day?

There was certainly no shortage of water today, it had started raining as the special thanksgiving service, at the Cathedral, got underway at 2.15pm. Hundreds were there to join in and listen to the Bishop's address, the hymns, the psalms, the lessons and the sermon, a water message in all and finishing with the blessing.

The congregation filed out followed by the Civic Party and their guests, the band marched off, escorting all along Lindum Terrace and arriving at 3.30pm in the Arboretum. This was the day to turn on the new water supply, but nature wasn't to be out done, the heavens opened, everyone, including the thousands waiting at the Arboretum, were soaked.

The rain continued as the speeches began, the Town Clerk, Mr W T Page, was the first up, he talked about the last 70 years, the efforts, the successes, the misfortunes and the disappointment of the Boultham Bore, he said the bore though was not to be a complete waste, a new swimming baths, on the site, was planned and it was to be supplied by the water from the bore.

He continued by explaining the actions of the last 6 years, the options available and the Elkesley Scheme coming together and how the scheme had cost less than the estimate and came in at £228,000, but that Boultham and the open reservoirs needed £80,000 spending on them to terminate their use. Which brought him into saying "overall each citizen would need to pay more for their water than that originally suggested", (more on rates later). With that, he paid high tribute to the industry and ability of Mr Barron and the energy of successive Mayors since 1905 to make this day possible, he thanked all others for their tireless efforts to the scheme and sat down.

Mr Barron was next to stand, receiving loud cheers and applause, he simply said he had only one or two points to add, one being that one full year had been used to prove the source for quality and quantity and 2 years had been used to construct the system and this had not been long enough to complete the reservoir. With the weather cold now the old open reservoir on Cross O Cliff Hill, could still be used without affecting water quality, until the new one was completed, but he hoped that if a few small fish were drawn from here, people would not

To Fetch a Pail of Water

think they came all the way from Elkesley.

He continued by explaining how water would enter the City via Westgate and flow through the City mains to the reservoir, he added how the quality had been declared as some of the best to be found, anywhere! He added that the scheme would be cheap to run and that which ever way the City was to extend, a water supply would be always be available, (How right he was).

Mr Barron then turned and from a tap he filled a silver goblet, turning and handing it to the Mayor asking if he would, before handing the water to the citizens, taste the water? The Mayor took up the vessel in both hands, drank slowly and long and then said "Citizens of Lincoln, I pronounce it very good indeed and I drink to the health of Lincoln, to Lincoln's new water supply and the continued prosperity of the City. "Mr Barron replying, said "The first drink of Elkesley Water has been taken in the City of Lincoln and I hope sir you will keep this goblet as a memento."

Mr Barron then turned to the Mayor and asked "Sir, may I now ask if you would show the citizens the water that has been brought to the City from Elkesley?"

Thousands of heads turned to the silver plated spindle cock on the platform and directed by Mr Barron, the Mayor turned it; a crackle and a splutter could be heard throughout the grounds, heads turned to the fountain, a single jet of water shot out of its highest point up and up it went reaching close to 100 feet, "the crowd broke into a choking cheer, so powerful was its emotion", as reported by The Leader.

The Mayor turned and cracked a second spindle and from a 100 orifices water gushing, gurgling and foaming, flowed from all sides into the two basins forming the lake around the fountain.

The Crowds watching the Fountain burst into Life.

To Fetch a Pail of Water

The excitement grew, no less in the Mayor, throwing one lever then the other, the water bouncing and dancing on its way, then the band struck a chord and many went into song "Now Thank We All Our God" as they made this the peoples anthem, many though sang and faltered with emotion, so happy and yet so sad, perhaps thinking of the past 6 years, was it finally all happening and could the City people now begin to look forward to happier and healthier times?

As the last verse concluded a large boom was heard as the maroons (cannons) fired, again and again, they fired and across the sky came parachutes of Union Jacks and another and another, once more and then silence!

A few moments passed then the Cathedral bells began chiming and as if Nature felt left out, the clouds burst open and down came the rain once again, but this wasn't going to stop the proceedings just yet. Mr Livens took the stand thanking the Mayor, the engineer and many more, more speakers the Sheriff (Dr Brook), Alderman Wyatt "offering sincere gratitude for the new water" and finally The Mayor with a closing speach, but it was announced that with the exception of the banquet that evening, the celebrations would have to be suspended and would resume again tomorrow, nature had had the last word after all. An oak tree sapling was planted, by the Lady Mayoress, with a silver spade, a simple ceremony a little way from the platform, only watched by a handful of people. With that the Arboretum celebrations came to a close, prematurely.

Assembly Rooms, Bailgate, Wednesday October 4th, 1911, 7.30 pm and by special invitation by the Right Worshipful the Mayor of Lincoln, The Citizens Banquet, was to begin."Anyone who was anyone, or had been" was there, providing they were men (The Corporation had decided no Ladies should attend. Though 2 ladies were there, for organising the catering etc).

220 diners, which included the Mayor, the Deputy Mayor (C.T.Parker) the Sheriff, the waterworks engineer and committee, the Lincoln Councillors, the

MP for Lincoln Mr C H Roberts, the Mayor of Boston, the Mayor of Louth, the Mayor of Grimsby, the Dean of Lincoln, the Lord Bishop, the Chief Constable, Magistrates, Corporation Officials, Consulting engineers, Medical Officers, representatives from most of the London and provincial newspapers, ex Mayors of Lincoln (C.W Pennell, J.W Ruddock, A.C Newsum, J.G Williams and C Pratt) and many other influential citizens of Lincoln. The Contractors to the scheme were represented, the Resident engineers to the scheme (Mr's Chamberlin. Mitchell, Horobin and Hewitt) and finally some visitors from another County who had recieved a special invite.

The banquet was preceded by a reception and at 7.45pm, the Chairman of the Meeting, Dr Mansel Sympson, lead the Guests into the, "charmingly decorated tables", dining area.

Some of the guests seated ready for the Banquet, all the finery as one would expect on such an occasion.

The Menu and programme of music

The menu was the first item of interest. It was shaped and designed as a replica of the Water Tower, it opened into a booklet and contained over 100 photographs of the scheme under construction, a written detail of the scheme, with some other notable items of the City, a full list of the guests, the programme for the evening and the menu itself.

With the meal completed the President of the Committee opened the speeches, many lengthy speeches followed, detailed, comical and sincere, many toasts, each followed by music and song. The President read out many letters of congratulations, of praise and of best wishes to the Citizens of Lincoln and the Water Works Committee. Next to speak was the Water Works Engineer, he

To Fetch a Pail of Water

Seen here, a 9 course meal that had been prepared by Miss Morley of the White Hart Hotel. (each person received a menu to keep as a souvenir).

thanked the many people involved in bringing the new water to the City and his mentor, who was at the Banquet, for training him and whom without this knowledge, could not have achieved such a Masterpiece.

Next was the City Member of Parliament, Mr C.H.Roberts, he opened with a phrase

"Water is the best of all the gifts, that heaven to man can bring
But who am I that I should have, the best of everything".

He continued by congratulating all and concluded with a toast. Many speeches, many toasts and many songs filled this unforgettable evening.

THE CITIZENS' COMMEMORATIVE BANQUET

THE *raison d'etre* of the Banquet is simply the outcome of a desire on the part of the Citizens to find a suitable medium for giving appropriate expression of their appreciation of the completion of the Work of the New Water Supply.

To this end the following Committee was appointed at Meetings convened for the purpose of considering the matter, and the result was a decision to adopt the means suggested, and to invite the Mayor and Corporation, and others who have assisted in the Work, together with the following Guests and Gentlemen of the Press, to assemble at this festive board, and to join with them in mutual congratulations on the accomplishment of this great undertaking

BANQUET COMMITTEE.

Chairman : WM. COTTAM.   *Deputy Chairman :* F. E. FRY.

BARTON, O.
BOND, The REV. REGINALD.
EPTON, R.
FOWLER, W.
FOX, C. J.

GRANT, F.
HALL, J. COLTON.
HARRISON, J. M.
PAGE, T. E. MAYNARD.
RASDALL, W.

RAYNER, J. P.
STEPHENSON, F.
WATKINS, W. G.
WATSON, F. P.

W. R. LILLY, } *Hon. Secs.*
C. W. PAGE, }

. . THE GUESTS. . .

The Right Worshipful The Mayor, Councillor CLEMENT H. NEWSUM.
The Deputy Mayor, Councillor C. T. PARKER.

Alderman HUGH WYATT, J.P.
  ,,   THOMAS WALLIS, J.P.
  ,,   EDWARD HARRISON, J.P.

Alderman MAURICE HENRY FOOTMAN.
  ,,   HENRY ALFRED COTTINGHAM.
THE MAYOR OF BOSTON (Ald JAS. ELEY).

Coun. WM. STEVENSON WHITE. Coun. FREDK. HOWARD LIVENS. Coun. MATTHEW HY. HOWITT
  ,,   JOHN MILLS.   ,,   WILLIAM OVERTON.   ,,   MERZA ABRAHAM ASHLEY
  ,,   THOMAS CHAS. HALKES.   ,,   THOMAS ROBINSON.   ,,   HERBERT ED. NEWSUM.
  ,,   EDWIN TEESDALE.   ,,   PEARCE MILNER.   ,,   GODFREY LOWE.
  ,,   WALTER HY. KILMISTER.   ,,   FREDERICK DUNN.   ,,   REYNOLDS SCORER.

The Town Clerk, Mr. W. T. PAGE.
The Waterworks Engineer, Mr. NEIL MCKECHNIE BARRON, C.E.

CHARLES H. ROBERTS, ESQ., M.P.
Sir ROBERT FILMER, BART.
CHARLES HILTON SEELY, ESQ.
THE MAYOR OF LOUTH (Ald GEO. BLAZE).

THE MAYOR OF GRIMSBY
  (Councillor J. WHITELEY WILKIN.
The Rev. H. H. CARLISLE.

EX-MAYORS.

Mr. J. G. WILLIAMS.
Mr. C. W PENNELL, J.P
Mr. JOHN W. RUDDOCK.

Mr. CHARLES PRATT.
Mr. A. C. NEWSUM, J.P.

The Dean, towards the end of the banquet, mentioned it was almost midnight and it was time to Toast the "Press", he acknowledge their involvement and added though it had been criticism rather than praise, a lot of the time. A response came from a member of the press, speaking for the majority, they thought it their duty to report on the typhoid disaster and the events that followed, but had viewed the passed few years with interest and sympathy, they were now trying to counter the doubtful impression left over the City of Lincoln, by reporting all was not only well, but that Lincoln had a fine water supply and something all could be proud of.

The City Sheriff (Dr. W. Brook) proposed the final toast to the President of the Waterworks Committee (Dr Mansel Sympson) and added that the President, had perhaps, never felt so proud as he did that night. The President responded briefly and the Banquet came to an end.

To Fetch a Pail of Water

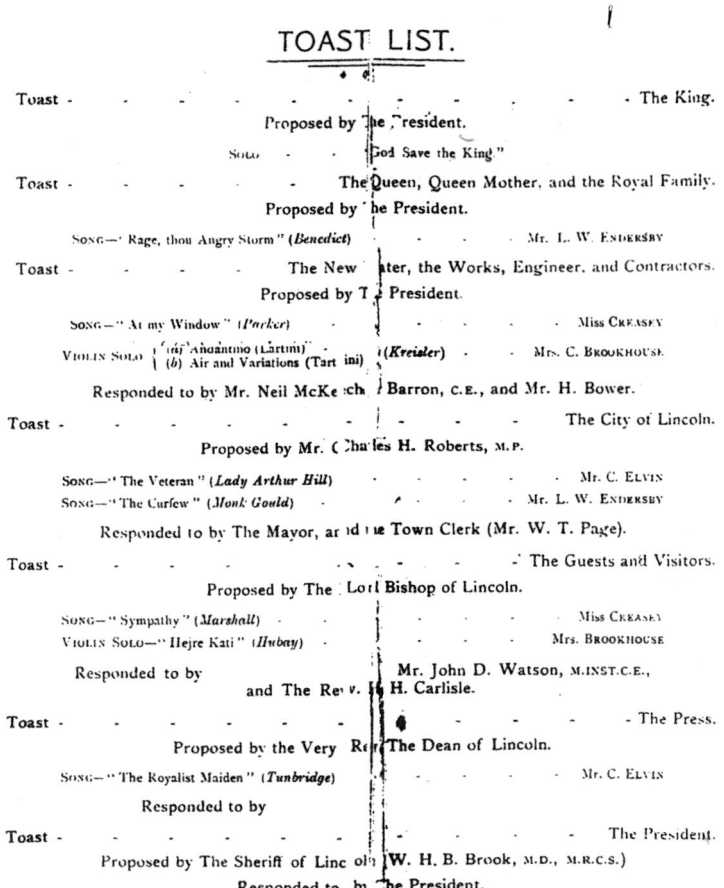

Order Of the Toast's

Left part of the Attendees List and above the Toast List and Proposer.

Thursday 5th, the rain had stopped by morning a slight breeze blew, the Arboretum and the scene was set for the celebrations to continue that evening.

Fairy lights were to be seen everywhere, Chinese lanterns swinging each side of the entrance, the "Great fountain", with its two basin pools brimming with crystal clear water, was lit up below the water line, the band struck up and played on and on and on. Thousands upon thousands of people packed, the Arboretum, all joined in the celebrations, "like a glimpse into fairy land", was how one

To Fetch a Pail of Water

newspaper put it, "has there ever been such a scene of so many amazed and delighted people", another newspaper pondered. The concert had been a brilliant success! The New Water had arrived spectacularly! Lincoln had not only got a good water supply, it had one of the best in the country! and the people, well, they were enjoying every drop.

Headline from "The Leader" newspaper
"LINCOLN'S NEW WATER
**Auspicious ceremony of the turning on.
A brilliant and prophetic success"**

A Great Occasion had come and gone, and would it ever be rivalled as one of Lincoln's Finest Hours?

Chapter 19
THE COMPLETION OF A MASTERPIECE

1912 An inspection inside the Reservoir shortly before it was filled to supply the City, looking above the heads you can see the electric lights, a must for the occasion as the covered Res had no daylight access.

The new water system was finally put into place, arriving in the City at the water tower, it passed into the tank through the large inlet main, supplying the uphill part of the City. Filling the tank, the water, returned down the second main into the City Centre Mains, up Cross O Cliff Hill out of the high level bellmouth at the Reservoir. Passing into the tank of the Tower to feed the high level area, then filling to the overflow level and finally discharging into the Reservoir through 8 inlet points. A second main from the reservoir outlet fell back down the hill to supply the Bracebridge and Newark Rd to the Lincoln City boundary.

The official of the Reservoir opening in 1912

The Reservoir capacity of 6,000,000 gallons, was estimated to be 3 days supply for the City. The small elevated tank (many passers by may think it is a chapel), allowed a water pressure higher than that of the Reservoir and so could supply properties at a higher level in Bracebridge Heath, Waddington, Branston and Mere and Canwick.

Many main laying schemes were also completed in 1912, bringing more areas onto the new water, those of Saxilby, Hardwick, Thorney, Newton and Burton villages were connected to the 21 inch diameter Cast Iron Trunk Main that had, until now passed them by. All could now have the same as the City, a constant water supply, either from the Elkesley pumped system or from the Reservoir if the pumps were stopped.

To Fetch a Pail of Water

Wickham Gardens

Though the water scheme was finally completed there still remained many items to be sorted. The reservoir at Westgate was cut loose from the drinking water system and a smaller water storage area formed within it, this formed the Wickham Gardens Swimming Baths.

A park was developed with a bowling green covering the remaining area of the old reservoir. Surrounded by a low stone wall with a twin railing gate, at the entrance from Westgate and a railing fence mounted on the low surrounding wall, running to a twin railing gate and supporting stone pillars, to form the entrance from Chapel Lane and all painted black with gold tops and fittings. Another stone wall was built across the front of the tower with steps up to an opening leading to the Tower's entrance, with each stone pillar, as at the Chapel Lane entrance, capped with a large stone ball.

The rain water drains from the Tower's roof, there were 4 (1 in each corner inside), were channelled to a common point at the basement of the tower and directed into a deep soakaway under the middle of the newly formed bowling green. The water tank overflow pipe was brought down and followed a similar direction, but this time it was connected into the old reservoir overflow pipe, this old pipe being traced to a ditch by the West Common on Long Leys Road, quite close to the Ornamental Pond (Posing the question, had its outlet originally, terminated at the pond and was this the reason for the pond?).

The Boultham filters were kept, as was the borehole and used to filter the clear water, white tiled, storage tank which was converted to form a swimming baths (the first of 2 tiled baths to be seen at Boultham), the baths opened in 1914. (and closed only a few years ago.)

Although, as can be seen, a favoured area around this time for bathing was a little further along the River Witham. The Goshes or was it The Boshes? near Dixon Street (there seams to be some debate). The Corporation had installed this area just along from Boultham giving the City a third bathing area.

The Old Reservoir on Cross O Cliff Hill was disconnected and used by the Mental Asylum for storage and for fire protection, they in turn built their own water system complete with tower, using the new water from the trunk main running alongside.

The Hartsholme Reservoir was separated from the Boultham system and opened into the River Witham at Altham Terrace (this open drain can still be followed today). The water main from the Boultham Works was cut adrift and a connection at the High St allowed a reverse flow to bring water to Altham Terrace.

The Water Department was now taking on staff, to work solely on the water system (all workers for the Corporation, up to now, would be general workers. ie.they worked on any department as req'd). The new staff were to form the plumbing section or as it was to become "the distribution section". This section was responsible for the mains network, the service pipes to each property, the fire hydrants and the detection and repair of leaks.

As well as main and service layers this department also had waste inspectors, the water was deemed such a precious commodity, that any leaks needed to be quickly investigated and rectified by these inspectors. This department would also replace, free of charge, any leaking tap washers in customers premises. A workshop was also set up and all the fittings to be used in the water system would be tested before being put into use. Further inspectors in this section would strictly control the plumbing trade, they would inspect all installations and only allow connections to the water mains if they met the required standard for by laws. They also had the power, through The Water Act, to disconnect or summon anyone who was in breach of the Water Bylaws. These men were important members of the department and were easily recognised by their uniform. A black suit, black tie and waistcoat, with a black coat and a black bowler hat. The hat carried a badge of the Lincoln City Crest with lettering "Lincoln Corporation Waterworks Department". Also in this department were the specialists, such as trunk main engineers, planning engineers and metering specialists.

The scene then was now set for many years of consistent and hopefully trouble free, water supplies to the City with equipment big enough to support its ever increasing needs for many years ahead.

Chapter 20
THE EVER INCREASING DEMAND

A little over 1,200,000 gallons of water per day was being used on average in the City, after the settling down of the new water from its introduction in 1911. In 1914, using the clause in the Water Act, Notts County Council requested an average quantity of 10,900 gallons per day, to be pumped to East Retford Rural District Council and during the war years even more was requested to support newly developing airfields along the route of the trunk main.

By 1919, Mr Charles Horobin had taken over as the engineer, the daily demand for water had increased to 1,700,000 gallons and although the water rate had remained at 2/4d(12p)in the £, a new rate for metered water was launched, causing confusion and chaos, but the Corporation were to persist with it for a further 3 years.

The Charges sheet, that caused all the trouble, issued in 1918

The water department got itself a motor car (second-hand), to help in a faster response to any fault in the system. The wages bill was increasing now with 9 employed at Elkesley, plus an extra man (part time) and 2 coal hauliers. Each works had a caretaker (Boultham, Westgate, Harsholme Res and Bracebridge Heath Res). Distribution employed 8 plus a part time labourer, an engineer, his assistant and 3 clerical staff completed the numbers employed. The annual costs,which included coal, maintenance to the system and works and general costs (insurance, petrol, rents, wayleaves, uniforms, clerical etc) was £25,000. There were incomes, apart from rates, allowances for those on military service for example, mains extensions, services and meters, both being paid for by the customer, bringing extra cash into the department.

A report on Customers Supplied read like this Population Supplied
Based on Estimated figures given at Enquiry into Boundary Extension 7 Jan 1920

Lincoln City	60,000
(not including Wragby Rd)	
Bracebridge	2,400
(2500 less 100 not connected B'bridgelow fields)	
Boultham Parish (2100 less 50 not supplied)	2,050
Bracebridge Heath Parish (30 houses)	130
(Asylum)	1,100
North Hykeham Parish (73 houses supplied)	314
Skellingthorpe Parish (59 houses supplied)	
(not including Swanpool or Hartsholme)	254
Canwick Hall and Dower House say	12
Saxilby (1 house)	5
Total Supplied	**66,265**

Figures based on an average of 4.31 persons per house

1921 the water rate was dramatically increased to 2/10d (14p or 14%) in the £1. It was back to 2/8d (13p) in 1922 and remained at this figure through 1923. These years paid off the loan, borrowed 50 years ago, when the Corporation bought the Water Company, also a loan taken 14 years ago as part of the Elkesley scheme loan.

During these early 1920,s much was being done to the maintenance of the Elkesley system. The bridges and exposed pipelines were being repainted, and an estimate for the painting of Dunham Bridge looked something like this...

"A gallon of silica graphite paint covered approx 800 sq feet
(say 90 sq yards) and cost .... 9/- (45p).

To Fetch a Pail of Water

The bridge req,d 2 coats(6450sq yards was its area x 2)
= 150gallons so 150 gallons of the paint would cost .... £ 67/10/0d (£67-50)
Six men @ £2-10-0d (£2-50) each a week
(12 hours per day for 6 days) for 13 weeks would could cost £195,
scaffolding for 13 weeks cost £60

the total cost = £322/10/0d (£322-50)
At Today's prices this total wouldn't pay for the weekly hire of the scaffolding.

Some other jobs carried out were...
Painting the tank at Westgate Tower, at a cost of £40
New tyres for the steam waggon, used for hauling coal at Elkesley £60
Repairs to the asphalt roof at the Reservoir and gunite lining of the walls ... £200
Clamps fitted on the trunk main at Dunham £130
The roadway at Elkesley was resurfaced at a cost of £350
The price of Coal had increased by .... 1/- (5p) a ton.

The chimney at Elkesley was heightened 20 feet, to improve the boiler efficiency.
A bathroom was fitted in each of the Elkesley cottages and DC electricity was wired up to the cottages from the dynamos /generators, one unit coupled and driven by each steam engine, this gave everyone DC electric lighting.

The Dynamo at Elkesley supplying DC Electricity to the site.

To Fetch a Pail of Water

In the Early 1920's a Committee of Lincoln Business Men, consisting of W.T.Bell, A.Bourneman, C.H. Newsum, C.W.Pennell, L.W.Smith, W.A Tritton and H.C.Wilson, requested a meeting with the Corporation, with a view to reducing public expenditure, the Mayor and Chairman of the Finance committee agreed a meeting.

Some extracts from the meeting

"Coal haulage costs are questioned, these costs were six times those of 1914 and amounted to 15% of the total coal costs (£3,970-11-7d), was this the best that could be done?

Elkesley roads and grounds, again compared to 1914 (£47-13-10d) to £593-12-7d, all buildings upkeep £230 to £939, Why so high? Could there be a saving?

The upkeep of the old Boultham Works at a cost of £178-7-9d per year, could this be sold off, as it was no longer of any use?

Inspections from £351-13-1d to £770, Was it necessary to test 5,200 bib and ball cocks?

Uniforms, are they necessary? A badge and card as 'bona-fides', should be enough proof to show the householder.

Salaries and wages are nearly equal, is there a reason for the high salaries level?"

All the questions were addressed and some savings were made.

1924 and further accommodation in the way of a semi-detached house was built at Elkesley, to accommodate more employees for the running of the plant. The steam engines were well into their stride although not really stretched and the output again had stabilised at around 1,800,000 gallons per day. Loans were being paid off now and the promise, over the last few years, of lower rates was made in a dramatic fashion, from a report, water rates to be reduced from 2/8d (13p) to 2/- (10p) in the £, but to help pay for some this the workman were to have a reduction of 1d per hour across the board, this would give a saving of £250 per year to the company". It was now claimed that "Lincoln not only had one of the best water systems, but was also one of the cheapest in the Country to run". In the report the Corporation stated it would continue to try to reduce costs still further. 1925, true to their word, a further reduction 1/10d in the £, a further cut to 1/8d the following year and yet a further reduction to 1/6d in the £ in 1927, the level to which it stayed for several years.

In the mid and late 20s many improvements were carried out. The spring / spa water was cut away from the conduits on Monks Rd and diverted into the Arboretum, with the spa being covered over at the Abbey, the conduits were subsequently supplied by the nearest mains pipe.

The communication system, using private telephone wires was updated. The engineers house at Elkesley and the Office at Lincoln were to be the central points for signals, fed from Westgate Tower, The Reservoir at Bracebridge Heath

To Fetch a Pail of Water

and Elkesley engine house. At each Centre a barrel chart was installed, with 2 pens (one red and one blue) for the 2 signals, these indicated the respective water levels in the Tower and Reservoir.

In 1911 at the Tower, remember the clock indicating water level in feet and inches, two wires had been fixed and every time the large hand moved through 6 inches a pulse was sent down the line, this pulse moved the pen indicator 6 inches and with chart marked off, in feet and inches, the level could be seen at a glance.

The Reservoir and now the pump could be slowed or even stopped at a convenient time without losing pressure in the system.

Into the 1930,s and the meticulous handling, sampling and testing of the water continued as it had now for some 20 years. In 1932 a sample failed its test, this triggered a search for the contamination. Many samples later and the chemists traced all the way back to the source at Elkesley without finding any pollution, some samples indicating E Coli a bacteria indicating organic pollution was present in the water. A report came from The Medical Officer of Health to The Chairman and Members of the Water Works Committee, confirming E Coli was present in the water and a report came from the medical officer of health to the Chairman and water works committee, confirming E Coli was present in the water "it should be looked on as excreta pollution was present in the water at one stage. It was not located and it was not felt the cattle grazing on the Reservoir was the cause, but they should be removed forthwith". The cattle were removed and the reservoir was isolated from the City mains, drained, cleaned and refilled with fresh water. On its return to service a chlorination plant, the first since the 1905 crisis, was installed to keep the water free from any further pollution.

1933 and a further sample failed, this again set the chemists, from the public health, off on a trail all the way back to the source at Elkesley. Tracing back down the line of the Trunk Main the pollution was suspected in the catchment area of the source, within a mile and a half from Elkesley. A Strictly Confidential letter from the Medical Officer of Health quoted "a test bore for coal was located and this was in the vicinity of some cottages, the sanitary arrangements of these cottages were not of the modern type and the sewage from them is allowed to run into a nearby field, close to the test bore, which had not been completely filled in. A definite danger of pollution, through the strata, could occur here.

The Report continued.."Also the method of dealing with sewage from the farm house close to Elkesley was not satisfactory and this too could be a source of pollution. Whilst it is not certain as to the source of the pollution, it is recommended that the whole water source should be protected by chlorination. I may add that the chlorination plant, already at the reservoir, should be kept as there is still a definite local pollution hazard here".

On this recommendation a chlorination plant was installed at Elkesley and a continuous disinfection process, of all the water being pumped, was set up. This was one the first of its kind in the Country and something many other water undertakings were to practice in the future. The Corporation were not going to be caught out again, the 1905 situation was still, after some 30 years, an embarrassment they still found hard to cope with, but it would never be allowed to happen again. The Corporation announced that "Chlorination was being carried out at Elkesley as a prophylactic and it would continue for all time!" (it did).

Continuing through the 30's, improvement and expansion was continued. Many more supplies were connected, many more mains were laid, a steady increase on demand for water was supplied. Nottinghamshire continued to take supplies from the City system and as Mr Barron had predicted, the pumps coped effortlessly. The only variables in costs were coal and wages. Coal, the more water pumped the more coal was req,d, the more coal used the more the haulage costs increased and so on.

Coal was bought equally by the ton as cobbles and slack, the cost per ton was, cobbles about 35 shillings (£1-75p) and about 20 shillings (£1) for slack and during the 1930's on average, the engines would use about 3000 tons per year.

By 1935, to a population of 69,458 in Lincoln 1,991,754 gallons per day was being supplied and 58,404 gallons per day to a population of 2,763 in Nottinghamshire.

At the Westgate Tower automatically operated electric pumps were installed on the City Main and if the pumps at Elkesley were stopped, then these pumps would start and maintain a level in the Tower by drawing water from the Reservoir.

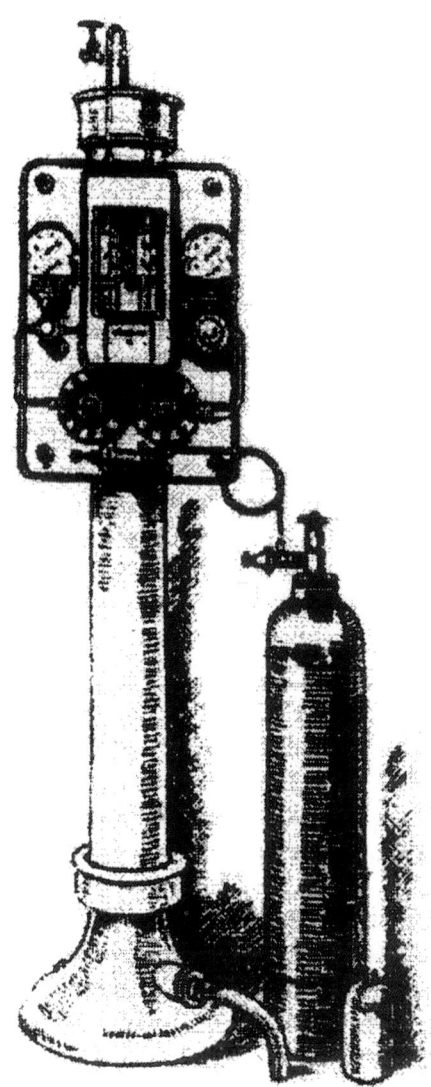

A typical Gas Chlorinator of the time

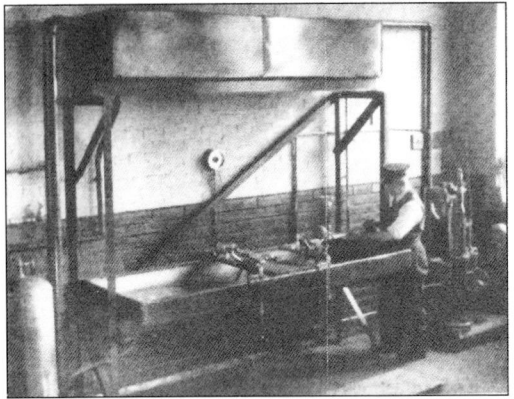

A glimpse inside the testing workshop at Stampend.

The Water Department continued to test all fittings and stamped them with the official stamp of approval.

Many pieces of apparatus were being used in the distribution system and all that were fitted below ground had a marker post describing what it was and where it was, its size and the distance away, from the post.

In the 1930's a fourth boiler was added at Elkesley.

Though fire plugs, hydrants and fountains (shown above) needed no indication as they could be readily seen and used.

Chapter 21
SUPPORTING BOMBER COMMAND

In 1939 an agreement was negotiated to supply, in bulk, water to Gainsborough Rural District Council Areas. Mains were also extended to join Welton and North Kesteven Rural District Council Areas Supplies to the Lincoln System.

On the outbreak of the Second World War mobile pumps, petrol or diesel driven, were purchased and with pumping points put in the mains at various locations, giving the option of moving water in either direction, should the need arise.

This picture shows one of the mobile emergency pumps in use.

Lincoln Corporation Water Department became the co-ordinating centre for the Waterworks Mutual Aid and after the bombing of Coventry, developed to an emergency water supply centre.

To Fetch a Pail of Water

This scheme involved the old works at Boultham, taking water from the River Witham with low lift pumps, into one of the old sand filters basins (now de-sanded) where coagulation took place (removal of solids). The open air swimming baths became the sedimentation basin, the baths pressure filters and chlorination plant were used for final treatment and as the water passed through them it was dispatched to a further, de-sanded, slow sand filter basin, this basin becoming the clear water reservoir. This works could treat and pump, with high lift pumps to the High St Mains, 1 and 1/4 million gallons of water per day.

As the War continued demand for water increased both in Nottinghamshire and Lincolnshire, addition bulk supplies were agreed with North Kesteven and Newark Rural District Councils and be it directly or indirectly, 8 additional Royal Air Force Bases were to be supplied, with a further 6 to be supplied as necessary.

In 1943, at the request of the Air Ministry, another borehole was sunk at Elkesley and an electrically driven pump was installed, this was to pump alongside the steam station and was capable of producing 500,000 gallons per day.

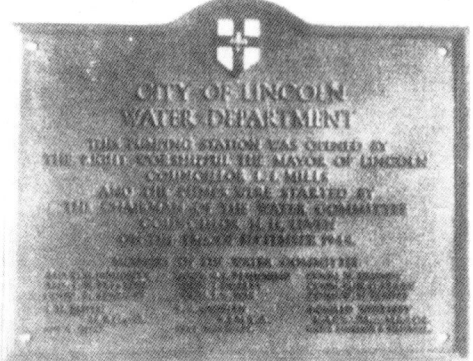

The new electric station at Elkesley.
The Tablet installed inside, Top Right.

To Fetch a Pail of Water

The view inside number 5 showing the electrically driven pumps, with the high lift pump on the left and the borehole pump motor on the bottom right, with the starters to the right and various measuring instruments at the back.

Above, Inside the entrance hall at the Reservoir with the new electrical control panel on the right, the steps leading to the tower on the left and in the centre the top of the spiral stairway leading to the valve chamber deep below.

Further work was needed in Lincoln to support the rising demand for water, the Tower on the Reservoir at Bracebridge Heath, was one part needing an improvement, as low pressure at RAF Waddington had been occurring, as this Airfield expanded.

Above, the automatic electrically operated pumps, installed deep below near to the main reservoir valves, taking water directly off the Trunk Main and pumping into the distribution mains systems of Bracebridge Heath and Waddington.

Also in the entrance hall was housed a pressure vessel, to ensure the water pressure was kept constant and the pumps could rest during no demand times.

During the war years the system suffered enormous demands, the steam plant was run on overload for long periods and many times over 3 million gallons per day would be pumped from it. It had not only come through unscathed it had supported more than it was ever expected to some 30 years earlier, this was truly a testimonial to its makers and its maintainers.

The Steam Station looking and working as it did on day one.

Chapter 22
THE CENTENARY OF THE WATER COMPANY

June 1946 and the Water Undertaking of the City of Lincoln was 100 years old. The hopes, the expectations, the failures, the good times, the sad times, the trials, the tribulations and the ultimate deliverance was, now, history. Lincoln had had, for the most part, a reasonable water supply system and since the introduction of Elkesley Water it had about as good a system as anywhere in the Country.

Water Rates were also 100 years old and comparatively very little had changed, the opening rate bill was 1 shilling and tupence 1/2 d in the £, it was now 1 shilling and sixpence 1/6 d in the £. Making other comparisons, much had changed; for instance. In the 1846 scheme the area covered by the water company was 17.78 square miles in 1946 it covered 222 square miles! The population served, in the first scheme, was 17,500 and in 1946 it was 83,000!

The water being supplied by the 1st Company to the City was 110,000 gallons per day, in 1946 it was supplying 3,107,000 gallons to Lincoln and 639,000 gallons to others, totalling 3,746,000 gallons per day.

The Distribution (pipework) system had been extended continuously over the 100 years and by 1946 the direct labour staff had laid and repaired over 150 miles of water mains. The Water Depot, at Stamp End, had been the Centre of operations for fittings and by 1946, 720 water meters had been tested here before being installed.

The original scheme had supplied 733 properties with water, many supplies were outside stand pipes supplying several properties, by 1946 most properties had their own indoor tap and many more had internal plumbing supporting two or more taps with flushing toilets. Over the 100 years, though, the 1/2 inch internal diameter pipe had remained the standard size for a house supply or service and each property had a water stop tap installed on its adjacent footpath. The first service pipe material was lead, by 1946 other materials had been tried, mild steal, copper and plastic, but still the preferred type was lead.

Over the last 6 years the water system had been put through its most strenuous trials yet and had coped admirably, those who formed the Company, those who reformed the system and those still involved with operating the system in 1946, could be proud at what had been achieved over 100 years.

The Inspectors had supervised all the plumbing work and repairs along with enforcing the "Water By Laws" throughout the City's water system, they had also continued to re-washer dripping taps, free of charge. The department's waste detection staff had continued to "keep the system tight", very little water escaped or leaked from the system with these inspectors about, they used what was called "The Deacon System" to detect leaks, but, I suspect, a good many of the leaks were discovered by the experienced ear on the trusty listening stick. (a cane with one end placed on the ground and the other end placed near the ear).

By the 1940s, the modern houses were getting a fixed bath in a bathroom accompanied by a wash basin and often a flushing toilet, there was also the "Wash House" with its large rectangular sink and wooden draining board. These rooms, along with the kitchen sink, would have cold water taps plumbed up to them. In the houses there was also a means of heating and storing hot water, the hot water was often plumbed throughout the house, this offered a whole new way of taking a bath, doing the weekly wash and washing the dishes, with a hot as well as a cold tap close at hand.

This photo shows the busy kitchen area, instead of the hand pump above the sink, there was a tap plumbed to the incoming water supply and in many cases a hot tap too. On the left hand side is the Aga Stove, filled with coal, wood or coke, it was capable of heating the house, the water and all oven or hot plate cooking.

To the left of the sink is the Dolly Tub complete with pegs, for clothes washing. Not shown, but a further item would often be seen the 'copper' it was also used for the weekly wash. It was a round copper barrel, with a means of heating, it often stood on legs with a removable lid. White clothes were put into it, filled with water and switched on to boil. Lifted from the copper, the clothes were put into the hot soapy water of 'the dolly tub', where they were agitated with wooden 'pegs' manually then rinsed & rung & hung to dry.

To the left is a washing machine, the lid would be shut, when the clothes were put in, the handle would be turned, rotating the rake inside, to wash the clothes. Lifted out with the tongues, shown on the back wall, the clothes would then be drawn through 2 wooden rollers, the mangle, where water was squeezed out.

Many tools were used on wash day, above is a Posher, it was put inside the wash tub and pressed up and down to make soap suds, or more of them.

To Fetch a Pail of Water

With the convenience of internal hot and cold running water and plumbed waste pipes to the sewers, water became an even more everyday household tool, which further increased the daily amount required. With this in mind, the water department needed to continually search for more water, by drilling more bores and to improve on the distribution system, by laying more pipes.

More sources were needed for the Lincoln System and with the "Bunter" Sandstone being the high quality water source, a further exploratory bore was drilled at Newton on Trent and after 1,250 feet an abundance of good quality water was found.

Artesian overflow from the exploratory borehole at Newton on Trent.

Elkesley was further improved with coal conveyers (left) being installed and (above) automatic loading hoppers to each of the four boilers.

More sources had come along on the outside of the "Elkesley Scheme", these were from the local limestone aquifer, which made the water somewhat harder in make up. During World War 2 the demand for water had caused much discussion and concern, so much so that in 1945 the government published a National Water Policy which quickly resulted in the Water Act being raised. This put all previous water legislation into a single act and much over the next decade centred around this Act with much rationalising of the water undertakings. The late 1940's and early 50's a new source had emerged at Newton on Trent, two deep bores had been drilled into the red bunter sandstone and these produced 500.000 gallons of water per Day, which was pumped into the nearby Lincoln bound trunk main.

Electricity was the motive force now in many places, but the two grand ladies of steam, at Elkesley, were still as reliable as they had ever been.

Over the many years of water undertakings, the water engineer was the key person, Lincoln had had many and all were very capable, but some had been exceptional, Mr Teague in 1846 and Mr Barron in 1908 for instance. And through the 2nd World War and into the 50's had emerged yet another, Mr Donald Whiteley, he had made Lincoln Water one of the leading water undertakings. He was appointed water engineer for the East of England and placed in charge of rationalising the East of England water area, as detailed in the Water Act

Chapter 23
THE WATER BOARD

April 1st 1961 and a new company was to emerge, it was to become separated from the Local Councils for the first time, Government backed, maybe, but Board run, the new way of operating the Water system was a new company "The Water Board". Mr Whiteley set up the new "Board", merging Welton, Gainsborough, Retford and North Kesteven Rural District Councils Water Departments, all merging with Lincoln Corporation Water Department and forming, The Lincoln and District Water Board. Newark Water was ruled out of the merger, after an appeal was granted by Government and Grantham Water was passed over, as it held a Private Water Company Status.

Virtually over night changes occurred, the Lincoln Corporation Water Department at Stamp End closed and re-opened in the, then recently vacated, River Board building of Aqua House in Harvey Street, Lincoln, (some of the Sobraon Barracks was also used on a temporary basis during the change over). The Water Office, on Lindum Hill, was closed, after many years of service and again transferred to Aqua House. All the merged Rural Council Water Departments broke away from their respective offices and set up in new offices, mostly in or close to a water works in the Area of the Council.

A whole new impetus was applied, on the arrival of the Water Board, all those areas of weakness in the system over the previous 20 years, were to be addressed and most of the systems that were stand alone were to be linked to support one another.

Potterhanworth had had a quite unique system for many years, a 50 feet (18 metre) high tower carrying a wind fan pumped water from a 100 feet (30 mtr) deep borehole, into a water tank above the houses in the village. This eventually gave way to an electrically driven submersible pump, which was installed in the bore, the tower was by-passed (it is still standing, but its use is considerably different today) and the village supply was linked to support Metheringham, Dunston, Nocton and in turn linked to Branston for this system to help support Lincoln or visa versa. Dunston had 3 boreholes feeding boosters at Waneham and as well as supplying Metheringham Village, this system supplied villages South of Waddington all the way a to a Reservoir, newly constructed at Leadenham. This system was connected to Waddington and Bracebridge Heath, creating a further input to Lincoln's ever expanding water system.

Many mains were renewed and many villages were to receive a piped water supply for the first time pressure, more security of water in times of drought, and an efficient operating system.

Villages to the north of the city received water from Welton, more on this later.

Elkesley Steam Station still playing the major part in supplying Lincoln's Water. This photo shows the rear and boiler house area, with its massive coal stocks on the right.

Throughout the 1960s water demand had increased sharply and the system was in real need of reinforcement. The River Trent Valley, now part of the Lincoln and District Water Board (LDWB), had been given a whole new purpose and name, Mega Watt Valley, here 3 coal burning Power Stations were to be built, which meant a large amount of good clean treated water was required and the LDWB were required to supply it. Although the LDWB had been used to supplying water to Lincoln's Own Power Station (ST Swithans at Stamp End) there was no comparison to the new task ahead, St Swithans produced around 60 Mega Watt a day, the new ones were one at 1000 and two at 2000 Mega Watts capacities. A new source was developed at a place called Grove in Notts this was to be the vital support to the Power Stations and any surplus would assist Lincoln City's system.

Electric Stations both for Borehole Pumping and/or booster pumping were being built along the A57 road to Lincoln and the Newton borehole source was further developed to house 3 pumps. The Cast Iron Main, for so long the only lifeline to Lincoln, was to get assistance, most of the section between Elkesley and over the River Trent was to be duplicated.

To Fetch a Pail of Water

Further development at Elkesley Electric Station, developed in the 40's, two more boreholes were to be drilled and a new Electric Booster Station, complete with a new section of pipe, giving it independence from its much larger sisters Livens and Janetta, the grand ladies of steam, barely a stones throw across the wooded hamlet.

This Station got a grand opening in keeping with a water source and was named after the Engineer, who for so long had made it all possible, Donald Whiteley.

The Elkesley Whiteley Electric Station.

During the 1960s it became apparent that a single input into Lincoln for its water supply and the Small Reservoir Capacity, only a little more than a days supply now, was too risky and it was thought reinforcement should be undertaken.So a large engineering task was unveiled, to lay a new steal Main to Lincoln, from the duplicated part of the Cast Iron Main as it came over the River Trent, this time though it was to run alongside the Doddington Road to the Reservoir at Bracebridge Heath. At the Reservoir a large excavation to build a second Reservoir, this new structure was to be two concrete cubes each holding 5,000,000 gallons, coupled to each other and coupled to the round existing reservoir, giving a total of 16,000,000 gallons holding capacity.

All was up and running by the late 1960's, 2 trunk mains supplying the City, up to 14 boreholes connected to the system, almost 3 days of storage in the City and electricity being the driving force for half of the 7 million gallons needed to support an average day's water supply to the City.

Chapter 25
THE AWESOME POWER OF STEAM

The identical twin sisters of Elkesley Steam Station were now into their 6th decade of pumping water into the City of Lincoln. Each had pumped a month at a time and withstood loading and demands far in excess of any of their designers wildest dreams

During their shut down period a maintenance routine had always been meticulously carried out, many visitors would descend on the site to see the steam engines in action, the Tag of "Lincolnshire Poachers" had disappeared and the two grand ladies had become the admiration of all.

Half of Lincoln's Water supply was still being supplied by the steam plant, the huge fly wheels slowly rotating with the whisper of steam jetting from various parts, the only telling proof that these engines were actually working, never a missed note and still performing as if they were installed yesterday.

Maintenance work on "Janetta"

To Fetch a Pail of Water

The crank of "Livens"

October 17th 1973, Janetta slowly and quietly pulsing the water to Lincoln on an ordinary winter's day, another School Party arrives to be captured by the splendour of it all, the engines spotless, shining and effortless as usual, the party go back to whence they came, another turn of the flywheels then suddenly a large bang and silence.

"Janetta" had exploded, a piston had been blasted from her insides, shattering the roof as it sped sky ward, 4 Tons of steal was on a route to cause insurmountable damage. A hole in the roof was only the start, smashed pipes, falling masonry and part of the piston eventually did find a resting place, buried in the top of a boiler, for so many years its energy supply, other fragments had wreaked havoc throughout the pump house.

Half the piston comes to rest.

To Fetch a Pail of Water

Taking 3 years to build, with 62 years of trouble free running, was this to be the one act that was to silence the steam plant forever? And was it to bring a premature end to this masterpiece of engineering? All was certainly quiet now, 30 minutes later No sound, No movement and No water.

The top of Janetta from where the piston had exploded

The Water Board's engineers were summoned to Elkesley immediately, not to assess the damage so much at this stage, but to find a way, short term, to get water to Lincoln. 3,600,000 gallons of water per day had just been halted with "Levens", the standby steam unit, unable to assist as it stood cold and motionless, her steam supply severed, her controls damaged and the building around her so badly damaged. There had, for some time, been an emergency plan to cover the short term loss of the steam plant, but no one had ever planned for this, this was going to take some time to sort.

The Whiteley Electric Station was now having to prove herself, to run at full load continuously, unassisted, for the foreseeable future, by her master in the distance cold, quiet and motionless. With the capacity at Bracebridge Heath Reservoir assured for at least 2 days, the Water Tower was the immediate priority. The source at Grove got a new sense of purpose, its usual Power Station commitment, but now, with the assistance of Newton and only the Whiteley Station, it had to fully supply Lincoln City with its drinking water.

To Fetch a Pail of Water

A View from the top of "Livens" soon after the dust had settled. Part of the piston finally coming to rest after demolishing the flow meter at the top left.
Whilst another part of the piston (bottom centre), complete with rod, trying to break through to the high lift pumphouse below, after demolishing the access hatch. The dynamo (centre top) through seems to have come through unscathed.

The view looking down on the Steam Station. On the roof of the pumphall is a rectangular sheet, this was the patch put on to cover the gaping hole, left by the piston as it was thrust into orbit after the explosion.

Chapter 25
A WATER AUTHORITY

April 1st 1974 Anglian Water Authority, along with Nine other Authorities, was set up by Government, it was to take control of water, sewage and river systems. Anglian covered from the River Humber to the River Thames down the Eastern side of England, some private Companies retained their status, but most Water Boards were merged into one larger Authority. A new Act, a new Company, a new Boss and now, for the first time, one company controlling the whole system of acquiring, treating, and supplying drinking water, treating the waste and discharging it safely back to a water course or River, not too far from whence it came. Or put another way, a man made water cycle controlled by one company.

Each function, Water, Sewage and Rivers, would continue to run with its own experts, though smaller sections did merge with their larger neighbour, Lincoln for its part, became the water centre for Lincoln, Retford, Bassetlaw, Welton and Gainsborough District Councils.

Meanwhile back to our story, only 5 months have passed since the explosion at Elkesley, electric pumps had been fitted down the deep wells, with diesel and electric boosters on the surface to dispatch the water to Lincoln, temporary maybe, but powerful enough to support the fast approaching Summer high water demand. At the Westgate Tower the electrically operated booster pumps were replaced and modified, this time they were to lift water from the incoming trunk main, from Elkesley, to the tank above, they were now vital to the system.

This system was to remain for the next 6 years, for after extensive tests and inspections it was sadly decided that as the "Janetta" steam engine was so critically damaged she could not be repaired and that "Livens" being of the same age could well come to the same fate. They would not pump water again, a sad end to the two Grand Ladies of Steam, reliable servants to the end. As a listed building though, it meant there was still further headaches for the engineers, how do they remove the engines to fit a new pumping system and leave the building in tact? Take a wall out, a window, the roof? The engines weighed, 250 Ton remember.

After many checks and many debates it was decided that the only way to restore a robust water supply system again, was to remove all the previous system and build a new one from scratch. Sadly it was judged that the engines could not be removed without the demolition of the whole site, though this would need Government approval, for the demolition of a listed building was a legal issue. A lengthy correspondence followed, in fact it was over 5years before demolition and a rebuild could be started!

The last thing to be built in 1911, was to be the first thing to come down in 1980, the Chimney! Many of the smaller items were removed and held in storage ready to go to various museums. The engines themselves, as part of the agreement to refurbish were found a new home and given to a trust with the view to "Livens" being restored, but alas this never happened, I guess the task became to great and expensive.

The demolition of the main pump hall, the stone carving, above the main entrance, was saved.

A new foundation ceremony was performed, with the original silver spade of 1908, by the Mayor of Lincoln and work commenced on the new pump hall. It was to be a fully automatic electric station with borehole and booster pumps, with No 1 Bore taking no part in this stations output and no settling lagoons for any red sand.

(It was calculated that little or no sand would be drawn to the surface as these pumps were to be fitted shallower).

The New Electric Station

The new Station was somewhat smaller than its predecessor, but it was equally as capable of producing near to 4 million gallons per day. It was also decided to call it after the creator of this water source "McBarron".

The loss of the Steam engines was not the only loss, jobs had also been lost and gradually over the 6 years, people had been retired and moved away from their homes in this wooded hamlet. The cottages were sold, as were the woods and some of the land surrounding the McBarron and Whiteley Stations.

Chapter 26
TOO LITTLE OR TOO MUCH?

Its been some twelve years since **To fetch a Pail of Water** was first published, and the profits made from the sale of the books went to WaterAid, the charity that works hard, world wide, to bring clean safe water to millions of people who haven't the know-how or the where with all, to find or acquire an abundant water supply to sustain a healthy lifestyle.

To enhance this revisited version, WaterAid has kindly offered for publication photographs of some of their work in progress throughout the world, our particular area being where water is scarce and the sanitation system is, well lets just say, little. Also the recent disaster areas of Pakistan and Australia, due to severe flooding and the earth quakes in New Zealand and Japan all who have had their drinking water systems severely damaged with many others being at risk of disease.

At the close of To fetch a Pail of Water, I mentioned the ever changing regulations, the ever increasing demand and the ever increasing pressure for water being a continuing problem. Twelve years later and this is still the case. But as water companies strive to improve the service they provide, the issue of leakage-and how to get on top of what is a never-ending job of repairing of bursts and leakage to pipes, has come to the fore. Perpetually shifting ground (natural ground movement), extremes of weather and the blunt fact of their age since they were installed, mean that many of the underground water mains that we have come to rely on are under more pressure than ever, both literally and figuratively. Its often only when we have this reliable water supply interrupted that we realise just how much we value it, as the work of WaterAid so clearly testifies..

The distribution network of water pipes has always been maintained to the best of abilities with the best materials available, but just like the water supply, it has expanded so rapidly that it is relied upon by more people than ever before. The materials used over the years for water pipes have been varied, and at the time of installation they were expected to last many years, cast iron, ductile iron, steel, lead, copper, plastic to name a few, all having to cope with internal and external pressures, corrosion and erosion. Over the last 30 years or so, much of the cast iron and lead pipes have been replaced or relined, with new poly plastic material pipes. Many of these new pipes have welded joints and are flexible enough to withstand much ground movement and large amounts of internal pressure fluctuations, but there remains a significant amount of pipe-work below our feet that needs replacing as it gets older and weaker. Corrosion and erosion as well as ground movement continually takes its toll. And with continued high demands, pressure has to be increased to maintain supply at all points. All of this means that leakage has the potential to get worse. Leakage is now one of the biggest problems in the industry, a major concern and a constant activity for the workforce.

A spectacular burst main and part of the excavation required to repair it.

Our water usage in every day life is still increasing and **an average person can use 30 gallons (136 litres) of water per day** just by doing the normal things such as hand washing, teeth cleaning, drinking, washing up and general cleaning. This 30 gallons includes about it 10 galls(46 litres) for toilet flushing (that's just 5 flushes a day).Other functions include 30 gallons(136 litres) for a bath, 5 gallons (23ltrs)in the washing machine.5 gallons(23 litres)in a shower and 4 gallons(18 litres) to prepare meals.

It takes 1 gallons(4.5 litres)of water to produce 1 Pint of Beer.
It takes 100 gallons(455 litres)of water to produce a Ton of Concrete
It takes 1,000 gallons(4,546 litres) of water to produce a Ton of Steel
It takes 6,000 gallons(27,276 litres) of water to produce a CAR

The use of water at our workplace has also increased. Water is used in the heating and cooling of rooms in almost every office, while the cooling of machines and, food processing industries consume vast amounts. Water is also used in the making of electricity, and in almost all manufacturing industries, shops and retail outlets. What's apparent is that we don't see all the, water that we use, but it all adds up today and everyday.

As mentioned at the beginning of this book it was written with the intention of raising money for the charity WaterAid. Before we continue the story, I would like to just pause and add a little bit of thought to get an understanding of the water on the planet and how we cope, or in some cases how we don't cope, how it will be in the years ahead, with our biggest fears of having too little....or too much, as with the flooding in Pakistan, Australia, Japan and many others. WaterAid are providing drinking water, helping to slow the spread of disease through the seriously polluted water systems in these areas, and in many cases training people to help themselves. In this section we will discuss the continued concern of coping and keeping safe this essential product.

Girl at a tap in Bangladesh
Credit Water Aid/Juthika Howloader

A Child collecting water in Ghana
Credit: Water Aid/ Jon Spaull

Water is life and without it there is no life. This says it all. Dinosaurs drank the same water that falls as rain today, and there's the same amount of water on the planet as there was when dinosaurs roamed millions of years ago. Natures Hydrological(Water) Cycle continues to convert salt water from the Oceans surface to fresh water which rains into the atmosphere and onto the land mass much as it always has from the beginning of life on land. Animals need it to survive as do humans. And, it needs to be clear of contamination and pollution to give all a long and healthy life.

The oceans and seas are all salt water and cannot sustain life for land creatures, and as all water originates from the seas, it is vital the fresh water is contained or

To Fetch a Pail of Water

restricted in its path from returning to the seas from whence it came. Nature to a large extent has helped with this by forming, below ground, impervious rock (non penetrable)and arranging on top of it a porous stone (a soft mineral rock, e.g. chalk, limestone, sandstone), that can absorb the rain fall as it seeps through the surface. This is known as an aquifer. It is like a big sponge below the ground where the fresh water can be gathered, in effect it's a natural large underground water reservoir. Some of these are confined and have no return to the salty sea, others have a return or overflow to the sea. Some have rain water sat on top of the salt water, which can be drawn off carefully as required, without damaging the seal (often referred to as the Saline interface).

Nature, by giving the fresh rain water a passage back to the oceans through streams and rivers, has formed large valleys in the Earth's surface allowing large lakes to form. These then are natural fresh water storage areas. Man-made lakes are also created by the damming of streams or rivers to flood an area of land to give a water storage area. These are known as catchment reservoirs. All the rainwater though cannot be caught and much of it does continue to try to return via any means back to the sea, though we do abstract again from these rivers to further halt its return.

Rivers though do have another vital role to play, and that is to return any surplus rain water along with treated sewage water, (nowadays treated to a very high standard), back into the salty oceans preventing flooding and allowing used water to start the cycle again.

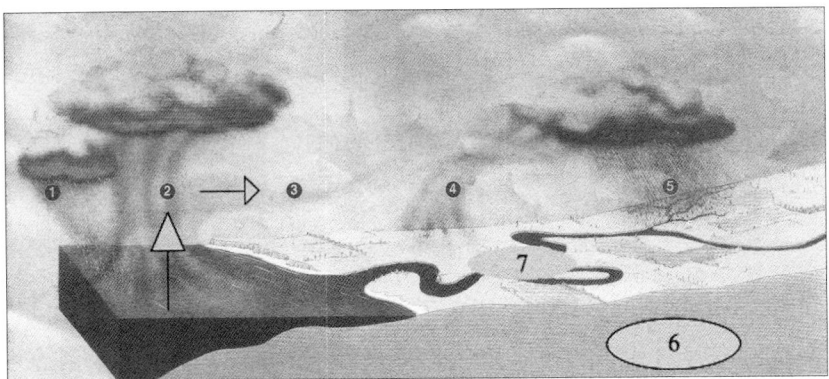

This is the water cycle, with the Oceans evaporation(2) forming the clouds and (1) the precipitation or rain falling back into the Oceans, as 70% of the Earth's surface is water then 70% of the evaporation falls back into the Oceans as rain. Fortunately the wind(3) picks up the other 30% and sends it over the land mass, picking up further evaporation (4)coming off the land, this then precipitates (rains) (5) onto the land further along. It then starts the long journey down and back to the salty sea, filling the lakes (7) on its way also penetrating the Earth's surface to recharge the Aquifers (6) below the surface. The Rivers, the lakes(7) and the aquifers (6) are the areas where the fresh water is obtained.

To Fetch a Pail of Water

Most of the water on the planet, 97 % in fact, is not suitable to sustain life on land. A further 2% is locked up in the snow and ice caps. This leaves 1% for growing all land crops, trees, plants and so on and drinking water for all land creatures. Though there is more than enough to go around, it is becoming less and less accessible. More pollution means more expensive treatment and we are using it more in our daily lives than ever before. With the worlds population growing, all these combined factors mean the fresh water is being used far more rapidly and the Natural Water Cycle could fall short if we don't change our ways.

It is possible of course to extract the salt out of seawater. This is known as, desalination, which is the man made version of natures water cycle. Desalination started in the 1970's in the Middle East in oil rich countries (it takes a lot of power). Today some 150 countries have a desalination plant. But it is very expensive to produce drinking water by this method, and it is therefore impractical in many parts of the world. As science progresses and the techniques change, who knows where we could be in years to come. There are new methods coming on stream each year, to produce drinking water from the salty oceans, and forward osmosis, biomimetics, and carbon nanotubes are some being trialled for use at the moment. These are new techniques and add to the standard method known as "the brute force" method, which uses membranes along with heat exchangers and, as the name implies, salt water is forced through the plant to make the conversion.

In the United Kingdom all drinking water is drawn from natural sources, either underground, or from the surface fresh water rivers, lakes or catchment Reservoirs, many of which are man made. All drinking water is piped and is available to almost every property in the UK.

This is quite unlike 46% of the world's population who don't have piped water to their properties, or even nearby. In fact some have to walk three miles or more to get their daily fresh water

Children carrying water in Kulunda, Malawi.
Credit: WaterAid / Jon Spaull

To Fetch a Pail of Water

Woman collecting water from an 'unsafe' dam in Ghana.
Credit:WaterAid /Jon Spaull

This is where WaterAid provides a vital support function. Over many years, volunteers have given their time to go to these remote places to advise and equip these people with the basic knowledge of how to gain access to a safe water supply. They help and show them how to find water, dig wells, fit hoists or mechanical pumps, and show how to dispose of the waste water afterwards, which is the cause of so much illness and disease.

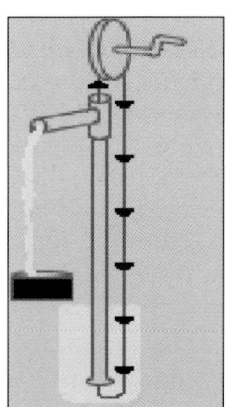

A Rope Pump, easy to install and operate.

5000 children die every Day from diseases caused by unsafe water
Credit Water Aid /Pada Diouf

A life straw provides clean and safe water by eradicating Typhoid, Cholera and Dysentery instantly and removing 99% of parasites, bacteria and viruses

Over 80% of London's drinking water is supplied by treated river water, chiefly the River Thames, where many other cities would have a balance of surface water and ground water. The wet areas, those with high amounts of rainfall, have large catchment lakes and man made reservoirs, but with large surface areas of water open to the atmospheric conditions they do suffer losses through evaporation. Surface water systems are also prone to contamination and pollution more readily than those of ground water sources. Surface water can also suffer more from taste, colour and odour, so these systems generally need more treatment and more protection than the ground water systems.

Ground water sources, or underground water sources as they can be known, are a lot safer because this hasn't the open surface area in which pollution or contamination can be accidentally created. It too can present taste and odour problems and it could be a hard water if its abstracted from a chalk or limestone porous rock. It may be discoloured due to the nature of the aquifer red sandstone or iron stone are very common sources. But generally it has a consistent character which means it can have a consistent treatment process. A problem with ground water is the activity on the surface, particularly at the outcrop (this is where the rainwater enters the aquifer). Here it can pick up contaminants, such as from farming activities, underground mining, even large excavations could effect the fresh water source, so this area needs to be protected.

Ground water treatment is varied according to the character of the water, but mechanical filtering is generally sufficient to remove most undesirables, where as surface water treatment(water from rivers and lakes etc.)requires screens or a sedimentation systems to clear plant debris and the like, and a coagulating system through clarification to remove smaller particles, soils and suspended matter. Some even require a biological process (this is natures own bacteria lending a hand). The water then goes through the same mechanical filtering system as the ground water.

Most drinking water treatment processes are a natural function with natural materials being used, filters use sand and gravel along with naturally formed resins/stone (garnet, anthracite etc). These are used to remove suspended solids as well as substances naturally formed in the atmosphere many of which may have an impact on colour, odour and taste. Granular activated carbon is being used extensively nowadays in water treatment, it adsorbs taste,odour, pesticides, insecticides and hydrocarbons, it helps with nitrate removal and it also helps to protect against any short term accidental pollution. Another new technique being used more and more nowadays is membrane, these remove all particles from the fresh water and return a crystal clear solution.

Throughout any water treatment process air is absorbed into the water by different methods. This disperses to the atmosphere many of the odours and accelerates the removal of some of the solids from the freshly abstracted water. It also increases the level of dissolved oxygen in the water (this is what makes it sparkle), it is a key part in the treatment process.

To Fetch a Pail of Water

A bell mouth method, water cascades and draws in oxygen from the atmosphere.

Hard water, and this varies enormously from source to source, is a different proposition. As there is a maximum high limit regulation on this it does need to be addressed at each source. Softening of the water is done by process treatment in many places. However hard water sources are often blended nowadays with a softer water source to get it lower than the maximum limit allowed. Lime scale is not as noticeable now as it used to be, but is still noticeable when water is heated or boiled. It can be a nuisance.

In the UK regulation dictates the maximum and in some cases minimum parameters of substances allowed in drinking water. This includes hardness, ph(the acid/alkaline scale),iron and so on. This is where the term "compliant" comes in and if the water is outside defined parameters additional treatment or blending with a compliant water is required to bring the water back into compliance. This drift out of compliance can be due to seasonal changes in the weather, high or low rainfall for instance. All drinking water sources in the UK are sampled and monitored continuously at source, with public health sampling being carried out, both independently and randomly. Samples are are taken and tested at regular intervals throughout the whole water network.

No matter what the source or treatment for taste, odour, colour, or hardness, there is one consistent measure that has to be positive at all times, and that is disinfection. All public drinking water in the UK is disinfected before it flows into supply. This is usually done by the addition of a chemical oxidant such as chlorine, chlorine dioxide or ozone and increasingly through the use of physical disinfectants such as ultraviolet (UV) light.

To Fetch a Pail of Water

Maintaining a healthy drinking water supply at all times is paramount. It is done automatically, and is fail safe, if the disinfection system fails or falls below the essential level at a treatment works then the water supply is shut off completely at source. This level of disinfection has to be consistent throughout the network right up to the point of use, usually the kitchen tap. It also has to be sufficient to protect against any contamination entering the system on its way to its destination.

Lincoln first introduced chlorine to the water supply as a disinfectant method in 1905, Lincoln was actually one of the first cities in the UK to use chlorine, but it was a desperate or panic measure at the time. Many methods have been used since and many methods are used today, Ultra Violet light for instance is very effective and is used regularly, though not in Lincoln supplies. A simple measurement of the level of disinfection at any given point in the system is required and chlorination offers this capability. This means that chlorine or its equivalent in liquid form, is still the main disinfection tool.

Chlorine doesn't come without its problems, though. Injecting sufficient chlorine to disinfect the whole system, but no more than is required, is a precise job. Water will quickly start to taste and could become unpalatable, not dissimilar to a swimming pool if chlorine levels get too high. A swimming pool has well over four parts of Chlorine to 1,000,000 parts of water, and drinking it can be very unpleasant. Whereas drinking water contains far less, in many cases, less than 1 part of chlorine per 1,000,000 parts of water. With disinfection at such a low level any adjustment required is so minute, 0.1 parts per 1,000,000parts, it requires a precise adjustment. However, even minuscule, and momentary higher levels of chlorine in the system could cause an unusual taste to develop, particularly when water usage, increases or decreases rapidly say early or late in the day.

This section has, hopefully, discussed what happens to the water in between falling from the skies and arriving at the tap. You'll also have some insight into how elements that rainwater pick up on its way to land, and while on land and how it is handled and how many of the elements are removed. The treatment processes are slow, but precise, and apart from disinfection to protect it from disease, the water arrives at our taps as fresh as it fell from the skies.

Water has many forms and uses, it is a liquid, it is a vapour, it is a solid, we drink it, we wash in it, it can be hot, it can be cold, it cools, it cleans, it changes temperature, it drives machines, and it cools machines, we can swim in it, we can drown in it, float on it, sink in it, it can be clean, it can be dirty, it is healthy, it can kill, it can be mixed with all materials to produce many solids, it feeds the trees, it puts out fires, it dilutes, it soothes pain, there can be very little and there can be far too much, most of all, water gives life, and without it there is NO life at ALL.

Chapter 27
A FEW PAILS MORE

In Lincoln the water supply was always treated as a precious commodity with wastage, leakage and metering being the priority. Washers on house taps would be changed for free, leaks would be repaired as quick as possible and metering was checked on a regular basis. Many properties were receiving a piped water supply for the first time as were many villages close to Lincoln, RAF Waddington, Washingborough and Heighington. To the west of Lincoln, the Elkesley system supplied Saxilby, Stow, Sturton, Newton and Burton direct from its trunk main.

The Lincoln supplies were the envy of many and villages to the east of Lincoln started to develop their own water supplies, some had a borehole or a well nearby and piped supplies to the properties were made with a local pump driving the water pressure. These pumps were often wind driven or DC electric powered. Branston had a series of wells that were piped to each other, allowing the water to flow from one level to another with a final overflow into the village beck.

Potterhanworth had its own borehole with a wind fan, like this illustration, as the power source for pumping the water. The water was pumped to a water tower in the village, and from here to the local area, Nocton and parts of Branston and Mere could be supplied.

In 1934 a new source was found and a well was sunk at Waneham Bridge near Metheringham, two Ruston and Hornsby single cylinder, horizontal diesel engines (65hp), were coupled through belts and shafting to two 4inch 4 stage Gwynnes(of Lincoln) pumps to run as duty and standby. Water was pumped through a 7 inch main to a reservoir at Metheringham Heath and then up to a

Reservoir at Leadenham supplying all on route. Also connected were two, 2 inch K type single stage Gwynnes pumps which supplied Metheringham village and Fen along with Dunston Village and Fen any surplus from these would flow into the Heath Reservoir.

It was found at certain times of the year that the well was insufficient so a shallow borehole was sunk 700 Yards away, near Dunston, and a Hydrostat pumping system was installed here, this was an unusual idea,though it had been used to some effect in Victorian times and maybe even Roman. Water was pumped down to force more water to come up, this system could produce 6,000 Gallons an hour, but it needed 4,000 gallons an hour to operate it. A 9 inch main was laid to couple this system to the existing system at Waneham, making this supply more reliable.

Early 1940's and due to the increase in air fields in this area, more water was required and two new boreholes were sunk, 150 feet deep, with insufficient water to cope with the demand a third borehole was dug 60 feet deep between the two and a horizontal shaft was dug connecting all three together. This proved more positive and in each deep borehole a Gwynnes vertical spindle, 4 stage 6 inch pump, driven by Electricity was installed. In the 1940's it was also decided to start chlorinating the water as a safety measure, this was to continue for the lifetime of the source.

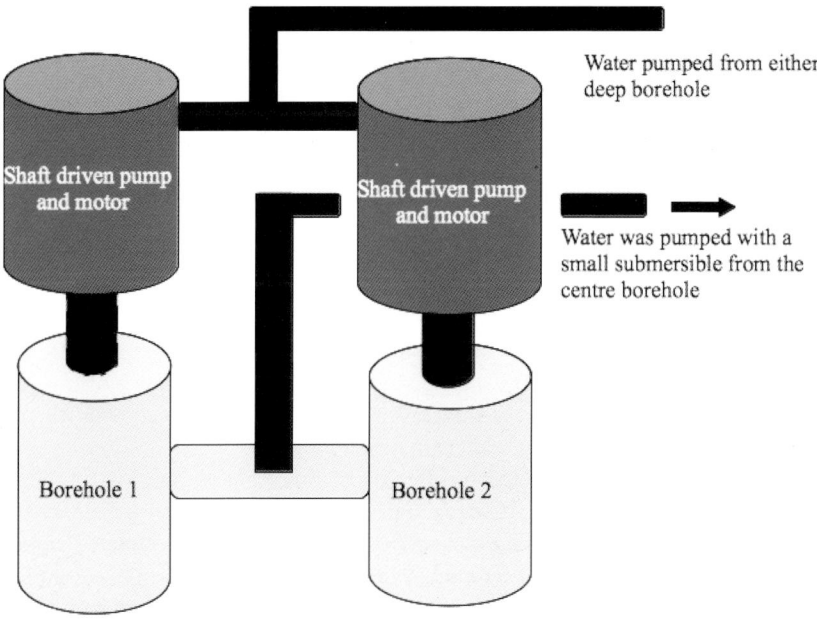

To Fetch a Pail of Water

The water was then pumped to Waneham Bridge Boosters, where it was boosted to the Reservoir on Metheringham Heath to supply the village of Metheringham and Dunston, along with the now larger Metheringham airfield. This supply was further developed and AC Electric pumps were installed at Waneham, with one running and the other on standby, they had two different outputs so that day or night conditions could be met. The supply continued to be pumped all the way to Leadenham 10 Miles to the south, where again demand for water was increasing, it could also release any surplus into the Bracebridge Heath Reservoir. The villages of Navenby, Boothby Grafoe, Harmston, Coleby, Waddington, Wellingore, Welbourne and Leadenham received piped water for the first time. They had previously had local supplies such as wells and springs, but now they had a good and ample supply, Waneham became an important source works for the South of Lincoln, manned 24 hours a day, because the system needed manual water pressure control, this manning ceased after electrical methods of control improved in the 1960's.

With Elkesley always keeping Lincoln in plenty of water, and with Potterhanworth and Waneham running continuously they kept the villages to the east and south of Lincoln well served and the Lincoln system was always there to back them up should things go wrong. As demand continued to increase the small tower/tank at BBH Reservoir was taken out of service and a pumping system was installed complete with a Pressure Vessel to give a more constant pressure, this upgrade was necessary to maintain a good pressure to RAF Waddington which had grown to became a major Airbase. The asylum or hospital for the mentally ill at Bracebridge Heath had also experienced low pressure after their own water tower had been taken out of service, so this again served their need.

As demand for water continued to increase, particularly with the increase in airfields in the area, both Potterhanworth and Waneham were called upon to produce more, and further sources were also being sort. Potterhanworth's single borehole pump was made fully automatic electrically and ran continuously into supply for many years, but water was being more scrutinised than ever and this source was close to the limit of permitted Nitrate levels and was eventually shut down when a new source was found. Waneham took on further supply zones when sources at Ashby, Digby and Scopwick were closed, because of quality, this was the Ashby Tower, Martin Tower and Billinghay Tower with all the villages within now receiving Waneham supplies.

Waneham's borehole water also suffered a high level of Nitrate, and although within limits it was felt it would be too high in a few years, but it was temporarily reprieved from closure and given a chance to test a new type of treatment, Nitrate removal, probably the first of its kind. Water from this plant was only used for test purposes and did not impact on the main supply, but it proved its worth, the plant did remove Nitrate from the Raw Water and gave the scientists a much needed treatment process to develop for the future. It became locally known as "Faulty Towers", after the TV series as this plant was a Tower with a lot of faults, but when it wasn't faulty it worked very well. Waneham pumped water into supply for many years and was eventually shut down after a new source was brought on line and because this source and Pumping station were in need of a major rebuild, being well over 60years old.

To the North of Lincoln it was a different story, the Lincoln system had enough water, but the Head or Pressure was governed by the height of Westgate Water Tower. Water could reach Nettleham but only just and the developing areas of Grange De Lings, Riseholme and RAF Scampton in times of high demand their pressure was very low.

Many areas had their own water systems, ie.wells, pumps, even springs, but in many cases not enough to supply properties direct, that is until a source at Welton was found. Two boreholes were quickly drilled at Welton and water was pumped into a newly laid pipe line to support the airfields developing in the area, Ingham, Bardney and Scampton. The water from here was very hard and caused a few problems when used in machines, the Air Ministry recognised this and asked for a softening plant to be installed, it was important to have a softer water to their bases.

A softening plant was installed in the late1930's (a Spircator system).

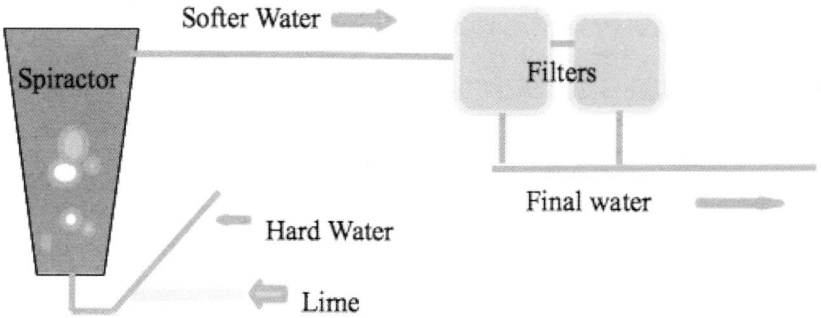

This softening process had a cone silo (narrow part at the bottom) full of fine grain sand, as the water was jetted into the base of the cone, lime slurry was proportionally injected, the combined solution then spiralled up the cone (spiractor) causing a chemical reaction to take place. This action displaced the Calcium Carbonate (limestone) in the water and the suspended particles wrapped themselves around the fine grain sand, building layer on top of the previous layer and crystallizing, much like a pearl. These "pearls"would continue to collect more and more Calcium Carbonate and would get larger and larger, eventually many "pearls"would be drawn off and disposed of. The water would then pass to a sand and gravel pressure filter, where any remaining particles would be trapped before passing to the storage tanks ready to be pumped into the supply system.

Hard water is determined by 2 parts temporary and permanent, Welton had 260 permanent and 200 temporary parts per million consistency. This spiractor system could remove most of the temporary part so a very effective softening plant was here, but it was expensive in labour and maintenance and occasionally the process would continue beyond the plant and a milky water could often appear at the customers taps. Chlorination at Welton was first installed in the 1940's.

A dual pumping system was at this Station (Works) supplied Welton, Dunholme, Scothern, Reepham, Fiskerton, Cherry Willingham, North Greetwell and on to Bardney, where a further Reservoir was built to support Bardney Village. From this reservoir water was pumped to a water tower in the Village were drinking water was also needed for food processing factories, vegetables and sugar in particular along with local dairy farms.

Welton's second supply system supplied water to RAF Scampton via Welton Village and into a Reservoir at Ingham, it could also pump direct to Ingham reservoir via Hackthorne Village. On this pumped zone Nettleham, Grange De Lings, and Spridlington were also supplied. From Ingham Reservoir the Welton Water could gravity flow from the Reservoir at Ingham Cliff to the villages of Ingham, Cammeringham, Brattelby, Aisthorpe and Scampton. Water was also pumped from Ingham reservoir to the Ingham Airfield and three water towers to supply the cliff villages of Fillingham, Glentworth, Hemswell and Blyborough, along with Hemswell Cliff airfield and a small reservoir at Harpswell Cliff. This reservoir was also supplied with water by a source at Glentham, which had been in use for many years supplying the local area. Harpswell Reservoir was further extended to support the airfield demand and an additional reservoir was built alongside to cover any short falls or losses, so important was this system to the Air Ministry. Water could gravitate from Harpswell Reservoir down to Harpswell village and all the way to Corringham where the larger Gainsborough system joined it. Pumps were also installed at this reservoir supporting the cliff supplies all the way back to Ingham Reservoir.

The Welton source was expanded over the many years, ten boreholes had been drilled on the site and two others could be called on off site, if needed, four spiractors were in use with nine pressure filters along with a large on site reservoir for storage. Another interesting thing with this water source was the rapid increase in aquifer recharge, during the winter months so good was the recharge many of the boreholes became artesian, this was the water coming to the surface, up the pipework by itself, this meant no pumping was required to get the water to the surface and it flowed into some purpose built storage tanks under its own pressure.

When the Water Boards were set up in 1961 Welton was in the Gainsborough Board area and the system was not linked to the larger Lincoln Water Board, so any improvements had to be engineered and funded by the Gainsborough

Board. In the 1960's the outer limits of this supply were beginning to suffer low pressures and no water, it was in a serious need of investment.

Bardney at one end of the Welton system, was one area that suffered on a regular basis and with Morrells, the vegetable canning factory and the British Sugar Beet Factory in the village continually losing supplies the situation had became serious. The school had no water for flushing or hand washing, some properties were off water for as long as 12 hours a day, and the abnormally low pressures had caused many hot water problems, that being none at all or too hot to use. The water pipes,or Mains as they were termed, were simply not big enough and needed replacing, but there were several miles of these so the task and cost was huge. Remedial work was instigated and a booster was installed at Langworth, it was to increase the pressure to Bardney, but it had to be carefully engineered as too much pressure would blow the main completely. There was a little improvement but many still complained of no water and much still needed to be done.

During the late1980's another Borehole supply was brought into Welton along with a supply from North Lincolnshire which was a softer water, the softening plant by now had come to the end of its working life,and as a softer water could now blend in with the Welton supply, the overall output would be a softer water. So softening was decommissioned but only after a new Rapid Gravity Filter plant had been built along with a new storage Reservoir and pumping system. In the 1990's a further expansion to this works allowed more water to be stored on site, along with a new source from the north, to blend with Welton and support the Lincoln system if needed.

The Welton works continues to expand it is fully automatic with back up generators to support any loss of electricity supplies and enough on site storage to supply the area and parts of Lincoln for a time. The villages named are still or can be supplied by this works though Nettleham is only part served, and Bardney is served from elsewhere. The Lincoln system supports the remainder of Nettleham and if the network was to fail then a backup is available.

The Water Boards throughout England and Wales in 1974 ceased and all water functions were put into ten Authorities, the Eastern part of England between the River Humber and the River Thames became the Anglian Water Authority.

In 1976 a new source of water was found and developed at Branston Booths. A single borehole to start with, it pumped water to a small covered tank 300 metres away, here the water entered at around 5 metres higher than the tank inlet and cascaded down a waterfall into the storage tank, aerating the water as it fell and allowing any gases to disperse safely into the atmosphere. This underground source was a little different to others, water arriving from rain fall, peculates through, settles or floats on top of the salt water that occupies the base of this aquifer, a natural barrier called Saline interface separates the two waters, and is

To Fetch a Pail of Water

the critical pumping level to which NO penetration should occur; should this happen the fresh water source would be lost and may not be recoverable.

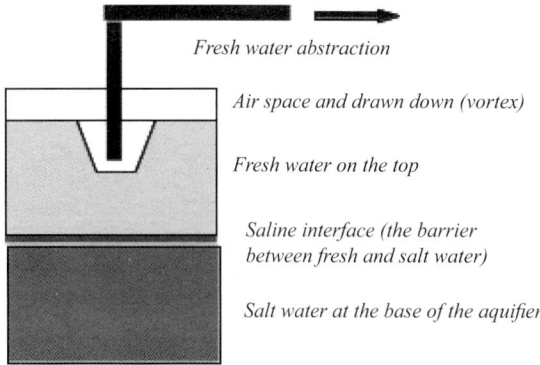

Fresh water abstraction

Air space and drawn down (vortex)

Fresh water on the top

Saline interface (the barrier between fresh and salt water)

Salt water at the base of the aquifier

Further measures to protect the aquifer from going saline were put in place, a constant sampling line for monitoring the incoming water, it alarms at a trace above normal and shuts the system down at medium risk level, a daily water sample is taken as with all the sites to be separately analysed. An electrode is also in place at the pumps suction point and on sensing no water it again shuts the system down.

AC Electricity had been used now as the driving force for many years, but speed control of an AC electric motor was not well practised, until the Inverter drive was introduced and this changed things considerably in the water industry. Instead of a fixed speed pump switching on and off with the rise and fall of a reservoir or water tower, now the motor speed could be adjusted by receiving a signal from a transducer(an electronic sensor), the sensor could be fixed to measure water pressure in any suitable location. So as water demand increased the water pressure would fall, sensing this the motor driving the pump would speed up and pump more water to bring the pressure back to its desired level, and visa versa as the pressure increased.

This type of drive system was installed at Branston Booths and for the first time in this area a pipe distribution network could have a consistent pressure throughout the 24 hours a day, and at night the pump would slow to nearly a standstill, due to lack of demand, saving on energy, but more importantly keeping the water pressure constant and also stopping the pump overheating during low demand times, which happened on the fixed speed system regularly causing high maintenance.

Branston Booths water is a hard water compared to Lincoln but is well within the required Maximum limits, it was further developed in the 1980's, receiving two more boreholes, and an upgraded pumping system, it was fully automatic, remotely monitored 24 hours a day and fully supported by electric standby

Generators. This source eventually took over most of the Eastern supplies of outer Lincoln, Washingborough, Heighington, Potterhanworth,and Branston. But this was also the turning point for Bardney which had long suffered from low pressure. A 9 inch plastic pipe was laid across the fields near the Causeway and a constant pressure was controlled within it. Fiskerton,Cherry Willingham and parts of Reepham,were also piped directly from this source with options for other villages in the area to be turned onto this network. If this Site was to fail, then a standby Electricity generator would re-power it and if the water Network failed then some, if not all, could be supported by the Lincoln City system for a time.

After a couple a years of this system being installed it became apparent something was wrong!

The Bardney 9 inch feeder main split from joint to joint on a full section of pipe(as seen above), cutting the water supply off completely to Bardney, and when this happened a second then a third time in different areas a reason had to be found.

The people of Bardney were again plunged into uncertainty over their water supplies, not the cause, but a problem was the variable speed pumps, supplying this main, would sense low pressure when a burst occurred, so they would speed up and pump more and more water into the main and of cause this extra water being pumped was just pouring out of the burst pipe, making a lake of water in minutes. A high flow sensor was fitted to switch the pump off should this occur again, and occur again it did, very often in the middle of fields with a full crop, this made it more difficult to find. The farmers having a reluctance to allow anyone on the fields for concern of further crop being destroyed this further hindered the repair but once found often the land would be so saturated,work on it would have to wait for hours before access could be made safely. Sometimes bursts were only found by walking down a field and stopping when it became very wet. Once the burst was repaired it was not the end though, as with all bursts it had to be sampled and tested to check on its quality or check the water was safe and not contaminated. The sampling techniques are very thorough and 100% positive, but it takes a full 24 Hours to assess, so this further frustrated those who had been off water for many hours even days.

The Mains were replaced from Langworth to Bardney reservoir and emergency standby pumps were installed permanently at Langworth and Bardney Reservoir. To be ready for any further emergency or loss of water from the Causeway side.

After much head scratching and many tests, it was found that the villain for the dramatic burst pipes was unusual ground movement causing a Bog Oak to rise. It is suggested this Fen many thousands of years ago would have been a marshland or a bog and it would have had hardwood trees (Oak)growing in it. In time these trees would die and fossilise, much like the fossilising of trees for coal, they fell onto the water table many metres below the ground, and just continue to move up and down as the ground moves.

Sometimes they come close to the surface and this is when the damage is done.

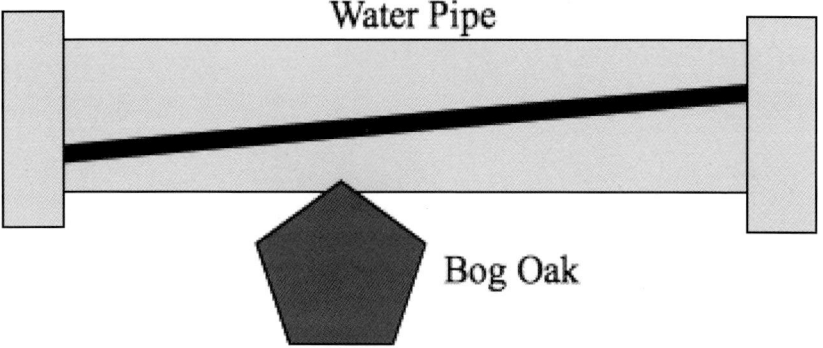

The nine inch plastic main was eventually replaced with a more resilient and flexible material pipe and positioned alongside the Causeway instead of across the fields, were it was at least going to be more accessible for a repair if it ever burst again, to date I don't think it has burst.

In the 1990's the site of Branston Booths was completely rebuilt, still using the existing boreholes, but Granular Activated Carbon Adsorbers were installed for protection of the source, this was becoming the normal at many source works in the 1990's, more on these later.

This chapter has tried to tell the story of the water supplies just outside the Elkesley system, which supports many of the villages, but also that they can combine to support each other and link to the Elkesley system if the need ever arose. Elkesley in turn could support much of this zone.

Today Welton and Branston Booths source works are fully automatic with enough water to cope with the need for the immediate future, the borehole water at Welton is blended with a softer water and provides a medium hard supply. Both sources, although not fully, can support each other.

Welton can support Lincoln via the water Tower and Branston Booths can support Lincoln via the Bracebridge Heath reservoirs. The Lincoln supply in turn can support, in part, both supplies.

Waneham is now Closed as is Potterhanworth.

Chapter 28
AND NOW ITS BEEN 100 YEARS

A Century ago the people of Lincoln had literally **"To Fetch a Pail of Water"**. The people of Lincoln had to get Government approval to draw water from another county. They had to plan, design, engineer, build and pay for a reliable, safe and consistent water supply some 22 miles away from their City. Such was the determination to prevent ever again disease or poor water entering the City's drinking water system.

From this... 1905
After the tragic typhoid epidemic, the only drinking water deemed safe was brought into the City by tankers pulled by horses and train tenders full of fresh water from nearby towns.

This photo shows people collecting water at one of the delivery points. This was a daily routine, for some this routine continued for six years, right up to the time the new water filled the City pipes.

To this... 1911

To Fetch a Pail of Water

The New Source in a Village in Nottinghamshire Powered purely by steam **ELKESLEY**	To the Water Tower in Lincoln **WESTGATE**	To the piped system of **LINCOLN CITY**

To this... 2011

A Centenary Celebration in 2011 to replicate the day the new water arrived in the City 1911 is to be held and it's not just about the City's water supply being free from diseases or its high quality or even its continuous flow for 100 Years, its also about the 100 years after a water source was born at a village in Nottinghamshire called **ELKESLEY.** Some 22 miles from Lincoln the source was designed, built and piped to bring clean healthy water to the City at a cost to its citizens and that it has flowed **NONE STOP** for over a century and still continues to do so.

The creators of this Elkesley System at its birth in 1908 carved into stone on the pump house
"AQVAE PVRISSIMAE FONS JVGIS CIVITATIS LINCOLNIAE SALV BRITATI MVNDITIAE FELICITATI DEDICATVS ANNO SALTIS MCMVIII"
which closely translates to "water as pure as the fountains of the ridge was dedicated to the joint health, cleanliness and happiness of the City of Lincoln in the year of salvation 1908"

To Fetch a Pail of Water

At the inaugural turn on of the water in the Arboretum, contained within the speech came these words "a system has been built to deliver the purest of water to our City, that will last 100 years and beyond!" Well how right they were! With the meticulous efforts of the workforce of the Lincoln Corporation, then of the Lincoln and District Water Board, transferring to become the workforce of Anglian Water Authority, to the present day workforce of Anglian Water, no matter what time of day or night, season, war or weather, they have successfully operated and maintained the system for over 100 years.

Elkesley has given a continuous water supply to Lincoln City and large areas outside the City, in some cases 20 miles away from the City, the Water Tower still functions as it started, the pipeline still delivers the same as it ever did and the source is still the main provider, though 100 years ago it was the sole provider.

How our predecessors would be standing with pride at this Centenary Celebration with the knowledge that it has not only stood the test of time, but also it has n**ever failed** to continually supply the City of Lincoln with its drinking water, n**ever letting the City go thirsty** and n**ever causing its people illness or harm.**

To appreciate the achievement of this engineering masterpiece we take a look behind the scenes from day one to the modern day and see how it has been used, controlled, monitored, maintained and has come through the difficult times throughout its 100 years.

The original works consisted of two triple expansion steam engines,each developing 450 Horsepower to drive two deep well pumps and one high lift pump. The steam came from three Lancashire Boilers, manufactured at Rustons of Lincoln. Only one steam engine could be fired at any given time, it drove 2 deep well pumps, suspended at 300 feet below the surface, and driven by overhung cranks at each end of the engine crankshaft, they pumped the water to the surface into small semi circular tanks where any suspended red sand particles would settle out. The outlet pipe from the tanks lead to the suction pipes of the three cylinders of the high pressure pumps, situated in the basement beneath the engine bed-plate, vertically below the steam cylinders. The high pressure pumps thrust up to 3,500,000 gallons or 15,820,000 litres of water per day to Westgate Tower at Lincoln 22 miles away, this was a lift of 420 feet or put another way 129 metres of water pressure. All that could be heard was the low sound of the two, 17 feet diameter and 17 tons in weight, slow moving fly wheels as the crankshaft was turned and just the occasional hiss of steam.

We have to appreciate 1911 technology, particularly when electrical equipment was in its early stages. D.C electricity was the normal power supply, batteries of today have this type of power and although very powerful it was limited and very difficult to control. Telegraph messages could be sent down wires to a set destination, and telephone conversations could also be made down wires again to a set destination. AC electricity supplies, the type we use in our

To Fetch a Pail of Water

houses today, were developing rapidly after its introduction in the late 1880s, but it was still very much in its early stages of development. Electronics, semi-conductors, electrical programming, radio control, remote control, silicon chips, computers, mobile phones and the like, had not yet been invented. Petrol and diesel engines along with AC electric motors were still in their early stages of function and control, but the mechanical control and movement of machines was very accurate and precise with it being logical and simple to operate.

The power source was steam, and yes many modern systems still use steam as the driving force, but the big difference today is the automatic control techniques. In 1911 the control was done by mechanical means, centrifugal force or hand adjustment, with the steam pressure capable of massive torque and power, very cumbersome, very slow, but very powerful and effective.

The Water Tower 22 Miles away was to be kept full, any overspill would go through the City Mains to recharge the reservoir in the South, but when the reservoir was full, any overfilling of the Tower would overflow to waste and although it would not cause any damage it was a total waste of time, coal and energy.

The water level in the tower was cleverly measured something like this; a tube the same height as the water tank positioned alongside, piped to each other, with the float balancing on the water in the tube. This was connected to a linkage chain, looped over pulley 1 and around the indicator drive wheel, then looped over pulley 2 with a balance weight fastened on the end for balance.

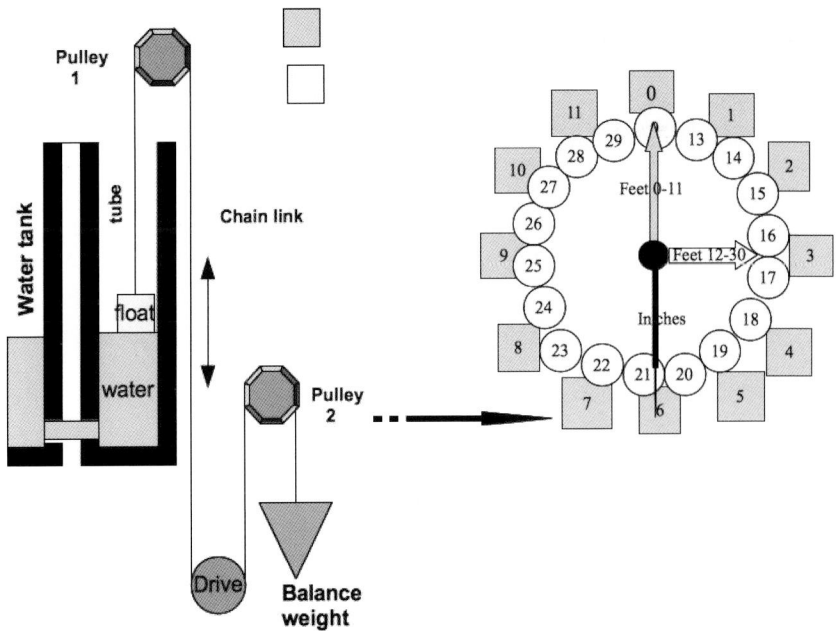

As the water level rises or falls the float responds and moves the chain over pulley 1, the drive wheel then turns and it is this movement that drives the hands on the clock face indicating the level of water in the Tank (16ft 6inches)

This indicator was at the Water Tower and with a series of low voltage relays connected to the clock, each time the water level moved 6 inches a DC pulse would be sent down the telephone wires to a similar indicator in the water office in Lincoln and to Elkesley Pumping Station.

The Reservoir at Bracebridge Heath had a similar Clock indicator, but this time the mechanism was an air bell, which worked like this;

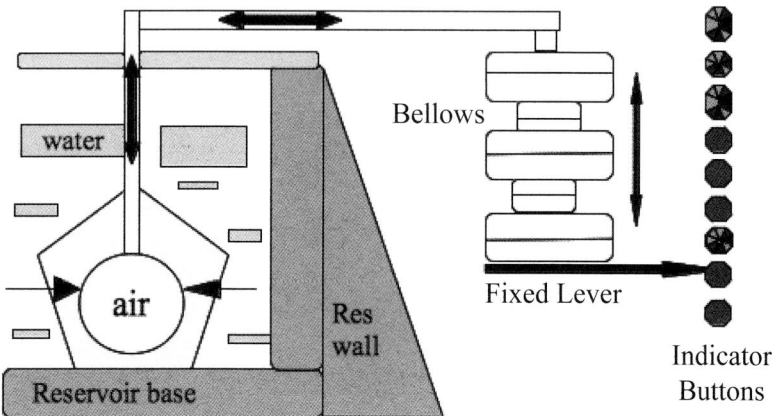

An inflated balloon, fitted inside a steel frame, with a thin tube fitted into its inlet and the other end of the tube fitted to bellows. With the balloon fully inflated and the bellows fully deflated, the air bell is lowered into the water, the water pressure will squeeze the air out of the balloon and inflate the bellows, the more water the more the air is squeezed out, so the bellows inflate in sequence and this moves the fixed lever up or down indicating the water level. Again this indicator was connected to a series of relays and each 6 inch change a pulse was sent down the telephone line to The Lincoln Office and Elkesley Pumping Station.

At Elkesley it was important to know if the level was going up or going down at the storage areas, so a seven day rotating chart with a clockwork drive was installed, it was all in a glass case and it looked like this...

These two indicators at the Elkesley Plant meant the engines could be operated as required, with maximum efficiency, no empty storage areas or any overflowing tanks..What is more these indicators continued to be the main control instrument over the time of the Steam Plant (62 Years) and were used until recently as indicators on the sites

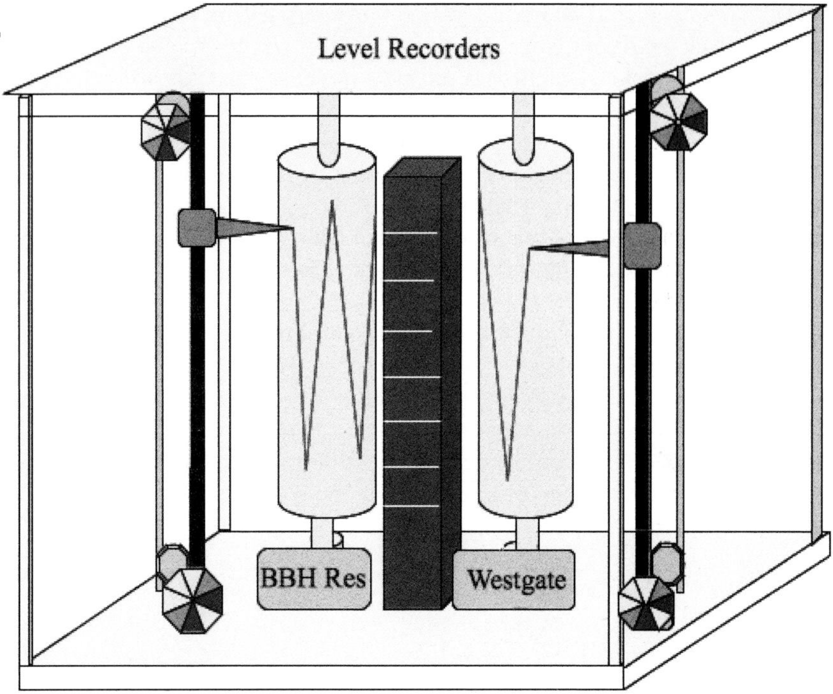

To Fetch a Pail of Water

Level Recorders

BBH Res   Westgate

A further piece of information was required for the smooth running of the plant, this was the water level in the aquifer below. To achieve this a compressed air line was fastened at the pump suction area, (a bubbler system) this gave a fixed measurement from the surface, with a fixed air flow pumped down the open ended pipe, by calibration, the amount of water above the pump suction could be measured, and so the water level below ground could be readily be recorded as well, this was known as Pump Depth below the water level. All so simple yet so effective in giving the vital information to keep the supplies flowing to Lincoln.

The staffing at Elkesley had to be an around the clock system of three shifts, essentially it was two man operated (an engine driver and a stoker) with a full time Maintenance fitter, and two labourers some of whom were also trained as stokers and drivers for cover of holidays and sickness. The site staff and site function was managed by the living on site superintendent engineer. It was his responsibility to keep the site functioning at all times and making sure it was properly staffed, a total labour force of 13 people operated the plant.

Within the licence agreement of the water abstraction from Elkesley, it was determined that all the villages and hamlets that lie in the vicinity of the Trunk Main feeding Lincoln, water would be taken off to supply these nominated areas. Several connections were made in the original plan and each needed a pressure reducing valve to prevent high pressures bursting the smaller local water pipes. A small reservoir at Tuxford was built to act as storage tank to help protect against any short term low pressure situations, the control of this was by a large ball valve, similar to the household ball valve used today in our toilets and cold water header tanks. Many villages came onto a mains water supply for the first time and this new supply was a welcome sight and supply to many in Nottinghamshire and because of the phenomenal engineering works a few miles away they have enjoyed a good water supply ever since, as for the works itself it took this extra demand in its stride.

Chlorine was injected into the supply in 1911 and has been injected ever since, the control nowadays is very high tech with the dosing being very precise. As water demand increased the Elkesley Works had to be expanded, the two ladies of steam stayed the same, a further boiler was installed, the chimney was heightened on a couple of occasions and automation was brought in as it became available. More housing was built within the hamlet of the Elkesley works so the operators could be closer to hand. The lighting throughout was powered by two DC generators and as the electricity systems developed to AC supplies, a public supply was connected and a conversion was made, though much of the clockwork operated devices and the DC controls stayed the same for more than 60 Years as did the two generators.

In Lincoln the water supply was always treated as a precious commodity with wastage, leakage and metering always being the priority. Washers on house taps would be changed free of charge, leaks would be repaired as quickly as possible and metering was checked on a regular basis. Many properties were receiving a piped water supply for the first time in 1911 as were many villages close along with the many airbases close to the Lincoln system, Washingborough, Canwick and Heighington benefited with a piped supply from this source. To the west of Lincoln, the Elkesley system supplied Saxilby, Stow, Sturton, Skellingthorpe, Doddington, Newton and Burton and various hamlets on route direct from the trunk main supplying Lincoln.

It must be mentioned again, as it was earlier in this book, what a massive part Elkesley took in the onset of World War 2. The Engineering industry had expanded throughout the Region to support the war effort, airfields had been set up just about anywhere there was a piece of level land and any land remaining

Part of an electrical control room, interior drives and programmable control systems

had become a food growing essential. And if this was not enough for the water supplier, then fire fighting must have also caused a lot of concern. If it did then it was well handled because Elkesley just carried on taking it, once again, all in its stride.

Then came the massive bombing of Coventry all their water supplies were severely affected, water supplies in the vicinity had to be diverted to Coventry, to fight the fires, support the industries and most of all to feed the population. Now, suddenly, a larger area was affected with little or no water available and this is where Lincoln was made the regional co-ordinator for water distribution, for the East Midlands and stepping up to the line was Elkesley. A new electric station with a newly drilled borehole was quickly constructed at Elkesley in 1943, pumping a further half a million gallons a day into the system. The steam plants output was put at full power day after day, after day, spare parts for the plant were made a priority delivery by the War Ministry, such was the importance of Elkesley to many at that time.

In 1961 the Lincoln and District Water Board was formed and Elkesley was by far its largest system, so much was focussed on its future needs.

In 1963 to cope with the ever increasing demand for water, a 10 year programme was put in place to expand the Elkesley system. Two more boreholes were drilled at Elkesley and a new electric station was built incorporating the borehole that had been operating since 1943, this new station was called the Whiteley station after the water engineer and manager of that time. The two Elkesley Stations together, could now deliver 6,000,000 gallons or 27,120,000 litres a day to Lincoln. The 21 inch trunk main from Elkesley to Lincoln was duplicated, in six phases (one short phase was not completed for some reason) with a 21 inch steel pipe, this would divert at Saxilby and go direct to Bracebridge Heath Reservoir, where a second service reservoir was being built to hold 10,000,000 gallons or 45,000,000 litres of water, which would bring this site water holding to 16,000,000 gallons or 72,000,000 litres, the whole programme was completed by 1972.

Original 6M Gallon Res.

New 10M Galloon Res.

The New Reservoir at Bracebridge Heath put this water holding into a different category of regulations, which meant it had to have a rapid realise system in the case of a fault occurring. This was done with two separate systems.

The first, should a burst TRUNK main occur, to prevent the Reservoir emptying into the burst a "butterfly valve" was installed in the Main and if the water flowed faster than the high flow setting off the valve, the valve would rotate from its normal horizontal position to a vertical position, closing the valve and stopping any more water flowing from the reservoir. The second measure was in the original design, but modified slightly, it also was to prevent a flood, but this time the water level was measured in the Reservoir and should the level drop quicker, after a period of time, on a pre set measure, then a signal would transmit to a solenoid on a valve by the River Witham where the trunk main runs alongside and this valve would open and discharge the trunk main and the reservoir water into the River. Drastic yes, but a safe way of preventing a flood from uphill Bracebridge Heath, not very good if you were on the river in a canoe! This nearly did happen.

To Fetch a Pail of Water

As a previous chapter has discussed the dramatic end of steam power at Elkesley was so sudden and completely unexpected, it took all the expertise that the Lincoln and District Water Board, soon to become Anglian Water, could muster to put in a temporary system powerful enough to keep Lincoln in water. Fortunately the time of year, October, was a lower water demand time, and the reservoir at Bracebridge was nearly full, but without a large electricity supply at Elkesley a lot needed to be done in a **few days** to stop the City going dry.

Elkesley was a hive of activity for the next nine months just securing a temporary system, it was a further six years before the new electric powered station came on line, because of the various objections to the demolition of the works. The Secretary of State for the Environment, after hearing all the arguments, in March 1976 made the decision for the demolition to go ahead and for a new station to be built. Once again the Elkesley water supply had come through a crisis and kept the City in drinking water with, maybe, no one even noticing.

The new electric station, was named McBarron, named after the founder and creator of Elkesley water, it ran together with the "Whiteley" Station the McBarron Station being the larger output and the major source, had 3 x 75 k Watt submersible pumps installed at a depth of 54 metres, they pumped water direct into the suction of 3 x High Lift pumps. These pumps were driven by 165 k Watt thyristor controlled Electric motors, the best technology of the time.

The site was capable of pumping 4.8 million gallons of water a day or 21 million litres a day, the complete works cost £600,000 and it was hoped this works would last for a further 70 Years giving uninterrupted service and to be a worthy successor to its Edwardian Masterpiece.

During the re-construction of Elkesley a new source at Newton on Trent had been developed, a new station with new boreholes and boosters were installed. This was connected to the trunk main to support the supply to Lincoln with demand for water always on the increase. A further booster station was installed at Whimpton Moor this was also connected to the Lincoln trunk main this drew water from another large source at Grove near Retford, which had been constructed to supply the Power Stations on the Trent Valley and support Retford Town water system.

With this new system, Elkesley, Whimpton and Newton, the water pressure needed to be lowered and this meant the pressure would be suitable enough for the main part but not enough to take water into the huge tank at the top of Westgate Water Tower. So in the basement of the Tower a pair of re-lift pumps were installed for duty and standby purposes. These were engineered so they did not affect the existing trunk main link to the High Street mains or the link to Bracebridge Heath Reservoirs. They switched on and off as the water level in the tank demanded. At the top of High Street two pipe coupling points were installed on the 18 inch trunk main this is the link main between Westgate Water Tower and BBH Reservoir and should the Elkesley to Westgate system fail a portable pump could be coupled up to draw water from the Bracebridge Heath Reservoirs and pump it to the Tower (the reverse direction of the normal flow).

Surely now this was enough to keep Lincoln in water for many years to come.

Well maybe the amount of water would be enough, but the water regulations in the 1980s now had to comply with European levels for substances in drinking water, some were for health considerations, (Nitrates etc) others were for a cleaner water (iron, manganese etc). These new regulations also had time limits imposed on them for when compliance was to be met. Elkesley fell into a cleaner water category and so treatment would be needed.

Remember the early Elkesley Water had a filter system to remove the red sandstone, these had been withdrawn when the new electric stations came on line because the water was being abstracted from a shallower position and, after meticulous sampling, no sand had been found, but now the problem was the naturally occurring iron, which is present in most underground sources. Rapid gravity filtration systems are capable of removing all the iron present in water. Stones, gravel, sand and various natural compounds are layered in a large filter bed, as water passes through the filter, the iron, manganese and other trace elements are blocked within the filter media. The filter, when saturated, is then reverse (backwards) washed and these suspended solids are pumped away for disposal. These, expensive to install, but cheap to run filter systems were the answer to comply with the new regulations and it was decided, because of location, that the Newton site should house such a system. All the water could be diverted into here, treated and then pumped back into the Lincoln system, but this also meant that the whole pumping system needed to change at Elkesley, Whimpton Moor, Westgate and Newton.

All the water flowing over Trent Bridge had to be diverted into Newton for treatment, then boosted back into supply. This was a major engineering project, that would need careful attention because Lincoln would still need to be supplied full time. The boosters at Elkesley were now oversized as were the Whimpton Moor boosters, because now the destination for all the water coming over the River Trent only needed to reach Newton and not Lincoln.

A New 36 inch Trunk Main was installed from Newton to Central Lincoln and the two Lincoln High Street mains were replaced or relined in preparation for the new system. Two new re-lift pumping stations were also to be built in this scheme, one to lift the water into Westgate Tower and the other to lift water to the Bracebridge Heath Reservoirs, with a further permanent booster station situated on the Lincoln City Trunk Main, to act as a safety system, to lift water into Westgate Tower from BBH Reservoirs should the re-lift pump to Westgate system fail. Some extra problems for this scheme were the Saint Georges Hospital supply it would need to have water pressure control and the new A46

Rapid gravity Filters

by pass road, about to be constructed, would cause a major trunk main pipe to be diverted, otherwise it would be in the way and finish too deep to be able to access it in the future.

Elkesley was refitted with new high lift submersible pumps in each of the four boreholes, with Number 1 borehole coming back into use, the high lift pumps were to play no more part.

This Newton redevelopment was massive in engineering work and costs, well over £30,000,000 initially and three years in the making, it came on line in stages as different structures became available, also the original 21 inch trunk main had to be cut for the first time in its history and diverted, during these engineering works, all these were a smooth change over with probably again no one even noticing. The Newton Water Treatment Works was opened in 1990, soon after the Company had been privatised, compliance to the EEC regulations was complete and the Lincoln Water System was once again set for a long service.

Arial photo of Building of Newton

The works at Newton needed to be robust, it had to have many fail safe devices as machines can fail and weather conditions can change quickly causing many problems.. Should the electricity supply fail, then automatically a standby Generator/ Alternator will start up and restore the operation and should this unit fail to start then its identical twin, sat alongside, would start and restore the system. Each unit had a 750 kWatt output and each are capable of fully powering the works at normal flow and pressure conditions, if necessary both would can run together.

An essential part of pumping water is surge, this is particularly dangerous when starting or stopping pumps, in most cases this action causes a reversal in direction of water flow and puts the system at risk of bursting or damaging machinery. Over the years a flap valve, a foot valve, a non return valve, or a reflux valve, all very similar in what they do, have been installed to prevent reversal of flow or mains emptying in the wrong direction, these valves usually had a huge block of concrete behind them to stop any movement during a surge.

An in-line valve was often used to control surge, at the starting and stopping of pumps this valve was slowly closed before switching off or slowly opened after switching on a pump. As more automation came in, higher pressures, larger pipes and higher flows, better surge protection was needed. This is done with a surge vessel, it is a large metal cylinder of compressed air coupled to the live main, as a surge occurs the air vessel acts as a cushion absorbing the water energy within it.

A lot has been mentioned about regulation and compliance, now another item came into consideration and that was future risk, particularly at the water source, ground activities above or below ground where ingress of substances (Mining, agricultural practices etc) could occur. These questions along with others brought more treatment needs to the industry. This further regulation

Typical pipework arrangement in a treatment plant

A granulated activated carbon plant

required further treatment to be in place to counter this risk by January 1st 1994, the water would be deemed out of compliance if it was not met. Various risks were deemed possible at the Elkesley and Newton water sources, pesticides, insecticides, hydrocarbons and other activities land based where ingress was possible, the treatment to remove these and many other trace items, was to be Granular Activated Carbon Adsorption.

This treatment involves tonnes of small GAC granules, of which the water would pass through and the substances in the water, would be adsorbed onto the surface of the granules.

Once again the engineers were occupied at Newton Water Treatment works with a £28,000,000 scheme installing six huge, ground level carbon hoppers and connecting them to the main works, all the water needed to pass through the GAC hoppers before going into supply.

January 1st 1994 and all was in place, the big switch over happened and apart from a few that suffered low pressure initially, all the needs were met, and once again, I guess, very few even noticed. A slight chlorine taste was experienced for a short time after because this new treatment process aided the disinfection of the water so the chlorine demand was less.

The Lincoln System is very high tech, it self monitors and it self controls every aspect of the process, as the demand for water changes during the day, then the system will speed up or slow down in unison, variable speed pumps will self adjust and are capable of pumping close to 900 litres a second. The filters will self adjust and backwash as required keeping the clarity clear and the chlorination in proportion to the flow making the disinfection precise. Should the chlorination fail the sites water flow will shut down instantly. The works has a self manufacturing chlorine plant which satisfies the disinfection demand and also eliminates the dangers of storing large amounts of chlorine gas on site. The whole Lincoln operating system is remotely accessible for monitoring and checking 24 hours a day also each site can be manually controlled on site if needed.

As the Millennium Year 2000 approached it became one of the most uncertain times for the City's water supply, as it did for all systems controlled by computers. Much was publicised about computer programmes failing due to the non recognition of year 2000, the information given was that computers had been set up by only using two numbers ie 1980 was 80, 1994 was 94, so all programmes would see 00 and it was unknown what would happen. Anglian Water spent a huge amount of money and time to try to counter the damage that could be caused, midnight December 31st 1999 and most Water Treatment Works were manned, just in case the unthinkable happened and everything shut down. Well either enough was done beforehand to prevent it happening or the whole thing was predicted wrongly, because thankfully, nothing changed and all went serenely on.

The only other cause for concern with this water supply was later in 2000, when a higher than normal level of the River Trent caused surging and flooding close to Newton WTW, an alarm was triggered and a shut down operated, an immediate plan of action was put in place, the works was sampled and tested. Precautionary notices were issued to boil the water before drinking.

Without hesitation all the water in the system was flushed to waste, samples were taken in many locations divers were sent in to assess any damage. The Newton Works was drained down, sterilized and scrutinised throughout, many more security shields and sensor alarms were installed and the works was put back into supply several days later. In the mean time the Lincoln system was supported in the north by the Welton supply and in the south by a combined Southern Lincs Supply, fortunately once again it was at a time of year of low demand. I think this event was noticed!

The Lincoln system, with the ELKESLEY source still the main contributor, continues through to the present day 100 years on, as does the Westgate Water Tower, the original pipeline, the Bracebridge Heath Reservoir, and most of all the healthy water supply that has kept the City safe for a century continues, just as did on day one.

A CENTENARY CELEBRATION of Elkesley Water arriving in Lincoln will occur on October 1st 2011!

Chapter 29
AND FINALLY

Nature continues to do the main part of producing fresh water from the oceans across the world and all land creatures continue to thrive on it, but slowly and surely the fresh water is becoming less and less available with pollution, contamination and wastage all taking their toll.

A lot has been said about regulation, better quality and less wastage and indeed a lot has and still is being done to address these problems, but the fresh water also has to be protected from over use and this is where another factor comes in. No industry or single person can abstract water from a water course without an abstraction licence. These licences are controlled by the Environment Agency, which is a Government controlled agency and their job is to keep a tight control on water resources and see that future demands can be sustained.

Levels and flows of rivers are monitored and can be controlled readily, in many cases by the release or restriction of water returning to the sea, whereas underground resources are measured on rates of increase or decrease over the year and are solely reliant on rainfall. The underground resource is more difficult to predict and some of these licensed amounts have to be adjusted each year to maintain a reliable water supply and save it from being over used. Licences have an average and a maximum daily limit that can not be exceeded, this again is to protect the source from over use or running dry and securing it for future use.

Year on year there is much competition for our natural water supplies, many industries require fresh water as well as the essential drinking water companies and the licences get ever tighter to protect against over use. The Anglian Water area, particularly Lincolnshire, has a less amount of rainfall than almost any other part of the UK, taking an average annual rainfall in central Lincolnshire of 25 inches compared to one of Manchester at 65 inches, so with less rain water available the tighter constraints have to be considered.

The Lincoln water supply system is solely reliant on under ground resources and a positive balance has to be maintained within the aquifer. The bunter sandstone, from where Elkesley draws its water, is possibly the largest natural underground source in England, but many other towns, city's and industries have access to it and they, like Anglian Water, are needing to think about the future. The Bunter sandstone at present is balanced and can support the current needs, but in the future any increase in use could start to tip this balance.

It is our way of life that the more water there is available the more we use it, the higher the pressure of water the more we use it, the clearer and tastier it is the more we use it, but the more we use it, the more we have to draw it from the source the more depleted it becomes.

It was once said invest in land they've stopped making it! Well we can't make water either! so we must look after it.

Anglian Water, over the past 30 Years, has developed surface water storage areas to support the underground resources that for so long have been the "back bone" for drinking water supplies. Huge man made reservoirs such as Rutland and Grafham reservoirs have been created they are supplied by rivers, boreholes and streams to maintain average levels, though evaporation takes its toll on these large surface areas they can be visually controlled. Many places are now using the rivers and waterways to support the underground sources and in many places it is becoming the main supply.

Getting back to the Lincoln supply system, the water quality is fully compliant and currently it is engineered to meet the current needs, but a sustained hot and dry spell has shown that the aquifer supply is close to the licence agreement or put another way the source is at capacity.

So where to in the future? With demand expected to increase, we need to be more efficient in the use of water, or recycling the waste water over again and again or even restrict river flows to the sea still further, all are options, but are difficult situations to balance.

The River Trent at Cottam Power station and in the distance passing West Burton power station.

The immediate future can only be from a surface water source and this is where Anglian Water are exploring the possibility of using one of England's largest rivers the River Trent. This river is over 94 Miles long it supports many cities and industries, including 12 coal or gas burning electricity power stations, its volume is huge and it conveniently flows past Lincoln's Water Treatment works, here it could be abstracted from the river, treated and piped into the city supply.

The River Trent as a source for drinking water has been talked about for a number of years and this year millions of pounds are to be invested, by Anglian Water to construct a pilot treatment plant alongside the River Trent at Dunham Bridge with a view to making this a support supply for the City. It is to have the latest in membrane technology for water treatment, it will take a number of years to build and test, but hopefully will prove to be the ideal drinking water partner to the existing supply for many years to come for the health and happiness of the people of Lincoln City.

And so we come to the end of our journey 2000 years of water in the City of Lincoln, the good, the bad and the tragic times all behind us, with the future of the water supplies looking healthy and as a new source appears on the horizon to provide a sustainable, safe, clean and healthy water supply for the next 100 years just as Elkesley supplies have done for the past 100years.

And finally as the demand continues to exceed the source, each summer we wonder if there is going to be enough, our health and survival depend on it, our ancestors most probably faced the same dilemmas, so after 2000 years, I guess, we shouldn't be out of answers, but a little scratching of the head is still required just as it always was.

References

The Engineer. - October 1911.
The Centenary of Water in Lincoln City.
Medieval Lincoln - Sir Francis Hill
Middle Age Lincoln. - Sir Francis Hill
Victorian Lincoln. - Sir Francis Hill
Water and Water Engineering. - September 1911
Water and Water Engineering. - July 1921
Water Supply of Lincoln by Charles Horobin.
Lincoln as it Was Vol 1, 2 and 3. by Laurence Elvin
Lincoln in the 50's and 60's. by Laurence Elvin
Lincolnshire History and Archaeology. - Various Vols 1976 onwards.
Industrial archaeology - Various notes from 1976.
Archived Reports - Various, Lincoln and District Water Board.
Archived Reports - Various, Anglian Water.
Archived Log Books - Various, including some of Mr McKecknie Barron's Notes
Minutes of Meetings Held by Lincoln Corporation Water Department.
Official Report from Lincoln and District Water Board October 1973.
The Modern Plumber and Sanitary Engineer Vol.2.
Anglian Water News.

ADDITIONAL INFORMATION FROM....

Interviews with Mr Tom Baker - Lincoln Past and Roman Lincoln.
Interviews with Mr Laurence Elvin - Lincoln Past.
Interviews with Mr Maurice Hodson - Views of Lincoln Past and many photographs and chats with so many local people.
Research from many Newspaper cuttings.
Including The Gazette, The Leader, The Lincolnshire Echo and The Chronicle.
The Local Studies Collection at The Lincoln Central Library.
Lincolnshire Archives.
Lincolnshire Life Museum.

To Fetch a Pail of Water

Photographs reproduced by kind permission of:
The Lincoln Studies Collection, at the Central Library, by Courtesy of Lincolnshire County Council Education and Cultural Directorate.
Many other photographs supplied by Mr Maurice Hodson.
Illustrations, maps and sketches reproduced by kind permission of:
Anglian Water.

To Fetch a Pail of Water

To Fetch a Pail of Water

To Fetch a Pail of Water

To Fetch a Pail of Water